Work, Democracy and
Development

Work, Democracy and Development

Socio-psychological Monitoring of Organisations and Programmes

Prayag Mehta

Sage Publications
New Delhi < Thousand Oaks > London

First published in 2001 by

Sage Publications India Pvt Ltd
M-32 Market, Greater Kailash 1
New Delhi 110 048

Sage Publications Inc
2455 Teller Road
Thousand Oaks, California 91320

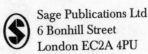

Sage Publications Ltd
6 Bonhill Street
London EC2A 4PU

Published by Tejeshwar Singh for Sage Publications India Pvt Ltd, typeset in 10/12 Baskerville by Asian Telelinks, New Delhi, and printed at Chaman Enterprises, Delhi.

Library of Congress Cataloging-in-Publication Data

Mehta, Prayag, 1926–
    Work, democracy and development: socio-psychological monitoring of organisations and programmes/Prayag Mehta.
        p. cm.
    Includes bibliographical references and index.
    1. Industrial sociology—India. 2. India—Ethnic relations. 3. Children—India—Attitudes. 4. Diversity in the workplace—Government policy—India—Evaluation. 5. Toleration—Study and teaching—Government policy—India—Evaluation. 6. Democracy—Study and teaching—Government policy—India—Evaluation. 7. Child development—Government policy—India—Evaluation. I. Title
    HD6957.I5 M433   306'.0954—dc21   2001   2001019394

ISBN: 0–7619–9557–9 (US–Hb)   81–7829–043–X (India–Hb)

Sage Production Team: Anjana Malik, Shweta Vachani, Radha Dev Raj and Santosh Rawat

Dedicated to
NARMADA BACHAO ANDOLAN
and other
PEOPLE'S MOVEMENTS
for
DEMOCRACY and DEVELOPMENT

Contents

List of Tables

List of Figures

Preface

The book has evolved over several years. The primary stimulus for the present work were the communal riots occurring from time to time in different parts of the country, notably in Gujarat and Maharashtra. An effort, then, was made to conduct research to develop a communication strategy for educating children, concerned functionaries and members of the public for combating communalism. Some psychological instruments were then prepared in this connection. Some of which, later further developed, are included here. Similarly, while working with industry and development programmes, it was found that one of the important reasons for poor performance were the values, attitudes and behaviour of the concerned functionaries. Some behavioural tendencies which come in the way of effective implementation of development have been discussed earlier in my book, *Psychological Strategy for Alternative Human Development: India's Performance Since Independence.* Instruments for measuring leadership values and problem solving behaviour reported, in the present work, were developed to address some such needs. The field experience also suggested an imperative need to locate development—rural, social and industrial—in interface with the overall democratic context in the country, where values, attitudes and tendencies play an important role.

A large number of persons and institutions such as school children, workers, managers, researchers and development officials have directly contributed to the present work. Particular thanks are due to the Indian Institute of Mass Communication, Department of Psychology, Udaipur University, National Labour Institute, Faculty of Management Studies, Delhi University, Division of Extension, Indian Agricultural Research Institute, National Literacy Mission and Participation and Development Centre.

Thanks are due, particularly to Pratibha Mehta for her insightful comments on democratic governance and development, and to B.P. Sinha, Neeraj Singh, M.L. Rao, Amin Reza Kamalian, Mahavir Jain, Preetam Khandelwal, Ashok Khandelwal and Arun C. Mehta for their help in preparation of the present work. Thanks are due also to P.N. Tyagi for his help in preparing graphs, and to Jagdish Singh and Satish Kumar for their painstaking assistance in preparing the present manuscript. Thanks are also due to the Editorial Staff of the Sage Publications Company, particularly Omita Goyal, Anjana Malik and Shweta Vachani, for processing the manuscript for publication. Last but the most important, this work would not have been completed without the unstinted support of Sushila.

I am grateful to all of them for their help and contributions.

Prayag Mehta

ONE

Work, Democracy and Development

Functioning of Administration: Dominative Leadership and Exclusionary Communication

A look at ancient society in India shows the importance of social theorising in promoting and reinforcing the roles of subordination and super-ordination. The social organisation was thus based on the notion that the society and the entire universe 'rested upon complementary and interlocking roles of different social orders sanctioned and sanctified by Dharma' (Kumar, 1986: 117–31). As Chattopadhyay (1989: 120) has remarked, 'the law-makers realised that it was not enough to enforce on the people their basic behaviour pattern with only the age-old provision of police and prison, the task became comparatively easier if, moreover, was enforced a definite thinking pattern on them'. Further, the dominant sections of society prohibited logic, reasoning and argumentation (*ibid*.: 117–18). They also prohibited Shudras and women from reading the vedas. The law books decreed that the social status of women was equivalent to that of Shudras (Basham, 1990: 104). Such an induced negative self-image was accompanied by contempt for physical labour. The whole host of socially useful occupations were labelled as socially inferior and impure (Chattopadhyay, 1990: 101).[1]

Legitimising the Colonial Rule: Inculcating the Colonial Mindset

Social theories, like the one mentioned here, continued to shape the behaviour of the dominant classes throughout history almost up to the present period. The ideology and image of the dominant classes as 'rulers' and 'superiors' for themselves, and contempt for the labouring people as 'subjects' and 'inferiors' came handy to the British colonial regime. They capitalised on the prevailing social conditions to induce people to intern-alise a self-image of 'colonised' and 'inferior'. It was a political expediency for them to establish their psychological hegemony and 'superiority' over the ruled. As Frank has shown, 'Europe was certainly not central to the world economy before 1800 . . . . In no way were sixteenth-century Portugal, the seventeenth-century Netherlands, or eighteenth-century Britain "hegemonic" in world economic terms. Nor in political ones. None of these. In all these respects, the economies of Asia were far more "advanced" and its Chinese Ming/Qing, Indian Mughal, and even Persian Safavid and Turkish Ottoman empires carried much greater political and even military weight than any or all of Europe' (Frank 1998: 5). It was, therefore, imperative for them to show off and legitimise their 'super-iority'.

The British could rule India only with the 'acquiescence of at least a sizeable and influential majority of the subjects'. For this, they used a 'powerful and plausible ideological legitimisation of their rule' along with brute force. They utilised the entrenched social organisation for this purpose. It was interesting in this respect that they promoted the Dharma-shastras almost as civic code which gave 'the pandits an unusual amount of power'. The colonial bureaucracy and the Brahmins thus 'struck up a sinister and complementary relationship' (Parekh, 1989: 15–26, 29, 31).

Functioning of Political Culture and Administration

Powerful historical antecedents have continued reinforcing political pro-cesses, policies and administrative tendencies after independence. The principle of super-ordination and subordination and self-concepts such as the 'rulers' and the 'ruled' seem to have got infused into our public systems (Mehta, 1998: 71–85).

Tardy and poor development performance in India shows the failure of the state and its faulty development strategy. Development has been mostly imposed from the above in the image of the top-down social organ-isation and the centralised system of administration. Besides faulty strategy, the related development functionaries have also contributed to such poor performance. The development mode, however, has largely been a one-way affair, as if people were static objects. Thus, instead of weakening, development in the country seems to have accentuated the dominance-dependence relationship.

Dominative Leadership: Exclusionary Communication

Such relationship informs the continuing history of 'exclusionary communication'. Soon after independence, the community development programme was launched (in 1952) with great publicity. Though it sought to enlist active cooperation and participation of the people at the community level, it was mostly implemented with a one way communication network. A paternalistic leadership style was used to diffuse messages, treating people as just passive clientele. Similar tendencies have been observed with regard to the vital programme of land reforms, implementation of Panchayati Raj Institutions (PRIs), and several agricultural and other economic programmes like Green Revolution and Garibi Hatao. If at all there were any interactions, they were mostly top-down, with the upper, more visible and dominant sections of society assuming the role of the communicator and the 'giver', reducing the people to the role of subordinate recipients. This, in turn, became an important cause for poor performance in the concerned development scheme.

Unilateral adoption of policies and their one-way implementation, ignoring the felt needs of the people, also goes against the principles of democracy, as these tend to cater to the interests of a few at the cost of the interests of many. Such strategies, in fact, show a low sense of empathy, on the part of the state functionaries, and low readiness to reach out to the people for stimulating and ensuring their involvement in development activities.[2] Under such conditions, even the decentralisation of governance and the PRIs, though important, would not be able to improve the quality of development performance. For example, there was no significant change in the provision of educational facilities in rural areas. On the contrary, the entrenched structure of dominance has tended to create a sense of insecurity among the teachers (Narain, 1972; Oad, 1989).

Exclusionary tendencies are also seen in the teachers' classroom behaviour[3] and the persistent phenomena of school dropouts and stereotypes in school curriculum.[4] For example, an elementary school level textbook in Rajasthan for civics contained a lesson where a teacher tells the class about a Harijan boy named Chandu 'look how neat and clean Chandu appears today, we should not hate him'. (Kumar, 1998: 72). No wonder, the Dalit, tribal and upper caste Hindu children learn to think negatively of each other (see Chapter 4).

Junctioning of Development, Equality and Social Justice

Such grossly discriminatory practices and negative social stereotypes are rooted in some of our traditional institutions which are still entrenched in our rural areas. There are instances where couples found guilty by the 'community' for going against traditional opinion were put to death, in some cases, by being burnt alive, with full complicity of their respective parents (Baviskar, 1997; Gupta, 1997, 1999). Recently, there was glorification and worship of sati (the practice of widow immolation on the husband's funeral pyre) with active participation of the wives of the Commissioner and the District Magistrate of the area.[5] Such episodes are planned to reinforce superstition and manipulate people's behaviour backwards.[6] Some educational programmes also, like vocational training courses, knowingly or unknowingly, seek to reinforce traditional gender socialisation (and discrimination) by stressing gender-specific skills like knitting. Similarly, there is a tendency to offer traditional craft and agricultural courses to SC and ST children, though the children themselves prefer learning modern subjects like science, english and mathematics (Shah, 1986). Such courses are also resisted by women, even in remote parts of the country, who aspire for modern skills which could help them in gaining employment and leading better lives. Instead, development functionaries from government as well as non-government organisations are found imposing their choices on the people (Mehta, 1995: 65, 147, 169–78; 1998: 124, 128).

Such manipulative behaviours are confined not only to the social sector but are also seen frequently in 'managing markets', particularly the 'capital market'. When a broker's connection with a stock becomes public knowledge, it is usually a sure sign of manipulation. Very often, brokers operate hand in glove with the company management. Such manipulative operations fool the investors the most.[7] Similar manipulative tendencies can be discerned at the state level. For example, the defence spending of Pakistan and India has increased by 14 per cent and 8.5 per cent respectively. At the same time, poverty has also gone up in the South Asian region. So also the income inequalities. Some people have become very rich in recent times through corruption. The region has the highest number of malnourished children, the largest number of illiterates, specially among females, with millions of child labourers.[8] There is unmistakable correlation between education and mortality rates, specially child mortality. A 10 per cent increase in girls' primary enrolment could decrease infant mortality by 4.1 deaths per 1,000 and a similar rise in girls' secondary enrolment could slash mortality among children by another 5.6 deaths per 1,000. Yet, such urgently needed development measures tend to be ignored (Dean, 1999; Mehta, 1998: 21–25; and UNICEF, 1999). Development policies and functioning of programmes thus show the officials' desire for dominative leadership over the people. They like to boss and act as patrons, treating the people as their subjects and clients—the recipients of charity and favours.

Exclusionary communication mode and dominative behaviour of development functionaries, including those in educational institutions (see Chapter 4 for functioning of schools), have thus greatly contributed to demotivating people and preventing them from putting pressure on the state and demanding adequate and proper education.[9]

The Emerging Psychological Change: The Changing Political Behaviour

It was during the freedom movement that Gandhiji established 'padyatra' as a mode of mass protest against authority. He wrote in *Hind Swaraj*, 'In India, people have generally used passive responses in all departments of life. We cease to cooperate with our rulers when they displease us'.[10]

In the last some decades, there have been several people's movements in various parts of the country around issues pertaining to environment, livelihood, forests, human rights, literacy and social justice. Smaller movements have tended to evolve into larger organisations such as the Kisan Adivasi Mukti Sangathan in Madhya Pradesh and Narmada Bachao Andolan (Bakshi, 1996). Such mass mobilisation has contributed to releasing and enhancing a sense of efficacy, a sense of standard in evaluating government performance and readiness for collective and individual action for various socio-economic goals (Mehta, 1995: 173–74).[11]

The changing public behaviour is seen clearly in the emerging competitive electoral politics. Active electoral participation and mass movements have the potential of changing power equations between the traditionally dominated and dominant sections of society (Omvedt, 1986; Rao, 1995; Sheth, 1996). Increasing people's resentment (at non-performance) and growing demand for accountability of those holding elective office, as reflected in frequent change of governments, is also a manifestation of the people's increasing consciousness (Satyamurthy, 1996b).[12]

The Dalit Movement: Democratic Upsurge

Mahatma Jyotirao Phule was an early social reformer who sought to make the Shudras (all non-Brahmins in Maharashtra) aware that their miserable condition was caused by the tyrannical Brahiminical order. He sought to educate and organise them for praxis for a more humane and just equalitarian order, and to prepare them to forge an alliance among the various groups of Shudras and ati-Shudras or untouchables, for such mobilisation (Auti and Chousalkar, 1986: 10–14). Ambedkar persistently emphasised political awakening and political rights, and the need for effective organisation of the 'untouchables'. He called upon them to actively take part in elections as a chance to share political power.[13] Since then, Dalits have come to consider political power as the key to their liberation. The growing political competitiveness and the new resultant socio-political reality could provide an opportunity for meaningful collective action for obtaining better public services and a better life for themselves. (see the section on People's Needs and Aspirations). This in turn generates a 'demand' for better performance and greater accountability from the state and other development functionaries.

Thus the turbulence throughout the twentieth century for democratic upsurge indicated the growing creativity and assertion among the hitherto subdued people. This resulted in the emergence of new centres of power such as women, Dalits, low castes, peasants and tribals, towards greater democratisation of society (see Mohanty, 1998: 63–81 and Omvedt, 1998: 223–41).

Increasing Electoral Participation

The changing mindset of Dalits is rather succinctly expressed in the competitive electoral political scene of the country in the 1990s. For the first few elections, the Congress party continued to dominate the electoral scene. By late 1960s, the traditionally backward castes started asserting themselves for a share in power and the electoral scene became more competitive. This period was also known for alliance among the Dalits, Backward Castes and Muslims. Such changes were seen more clearly in the 1996, 1998 and 1999 general elections. One defining factor of this emerging political scene was an increasing sense of assertion on the part of the traditionally oppressed sections of society. They appeared quite determined to win elections.[14] Another factor of far-reaching importance was that the Dalits were more interested in the democratic process of electoral politics than the socially and economically privileged sections. It showed fulfilment of one of Ambedkar's cherished goals, maybe partially, of the development of a new identity of Dalits (untouchables) as rebels, and its change from that of the 'meek and servile, uncomplaining and over-obedient'–'negative identification of being an untouchable imposed by the upper castes' to that of a 'positive self-image' (Gore, 1993: 199). Such a self-concept was also reflected in their increasing tendency (see the section on People's Needs and Aspirations) to judge the actual performance of their respective state governments and not just the promises, in terms of their own felt needs and 'standards'.[15]

Evolution of Political Behaviour: 1960s and 1970s

The changing political behaviour has evolved through the various protest movements and competitive electoral politics over the years, as mentioned earlier. Emergence of such changes was also somewhat visible in the political attitudes of the electorate during the 1970s. Most voters then favoured government control over industries and showed radical attitudes towards other economic issues (Sheth, 1971, 1975; and Roy, 1971). Studies showed that the real opponents of democratic functioning were likely to be less frequently those who have been continuously struggling for their primary needs. It was the alienated, educated people who were more likely to show greater cynicism towards the democratic system. Such educated persons were also found to show a higher need for authoritarian influence (Mehta, 1976d). As Kothari remarked, desperation and exasperation among the alienated elites could lead to a sense of ineffectiveness which may turn them more and more in opposition to democratic governance (Kothari, 1971).

Such growing democratic consciousness was an important factor in weakening traditional conservatism among people.[16] The disadvantaged were beginning to question the performance of the Congress governments as there was no improvement in their living conditions. Simultaneously, this period saw an increasing sense of alienation among the educated sections of society, particularly the youth (for example, see Sinha and Sinha, 1974; Sinha, 1974; Srivastava, Sinha and Jain, 1971; and Srivastava et al., 1967). Youth cynicism was stimulated by growing unemployment, weakening of the norms of public life and irrelevance of the education system itself (Mehta, 1971a). It was then concluded that, 'while the deprived and marginalised people were showing growing interest in electoral politics and in the democratic institutions, the educated youth were showing signs of normlessness and cynicism . . .' (Mehta, 1981: 607).

Political Assertion for Better Social Status: 1970s and 1990s

Though electoral participation provides political opportunity to the traditionally subordinated people, the built-in social and economic inequality works as a very strong inhibiting factor in their development.[17] With some improvement in their educational level and successes in the domain of competitive electoral politics, there is an increasing realisation that sheer numbers could collectively help them overcome the entrenched disabilities.[18]

More importantly, their voting behaviour shows that they are not willing to accept the role of the passive recipient and the pawn in the age-old environment of subjugation and subordination. A comparative study of their political, mostly voting behaviour during the 1960s and the 1970s on the one hand, and in the second half of the 1990s on the other, brings this out dramatically.[19] Another interesting change over this period is that the attitudinal differences between the deprived and the elite, as discussed earlier, can be seen more clearly. The enhanced faith of the poor and vulnerable people in democratic institutions assumes greater meaning in combination with their increasing assessment of their elected representatives. Thus, an interesting dialectical situation seems to be unfolding. On the one hand, we see the repeated rejection of state governments for their poor performance. It is confronted, on the other, by the continuing unresponsiveness of the ruling class towards the basic needs and problems of the people.[20]

The reason for such uniqueness probably lies in the social structure. The social structure has been a source of age-old oppression and humiliation for the labouring people. The unfolding electoral politics over the years, accompanied by development rhetoric and protest movements, has contributed greatly to the continuing battle for more humane and egalitarian society in the country.[21] As such an assertiveness has increased, so also has the alienation of the educated privileged sections from the pressing issues of society. It is now showing up in the reduced voter turnout from among them.

The Thrust for Democratisation

Measures for empowerment of people and their greater electoral participation, though very important, may not automatically lead to the democratisation of society. Formal institutional arrangements such as providing 33 per cent reservation to women in panchayats, may also not necessarily eliminate the prevailing unequal power and social structures. As the existing social structures are based on ingrained inequality, they can only inhibit rather than promote new egalitarian relationships. If democracy is to solve people's problems, then it has to concern itself with such needs of the poor as education, literacy, health and nutrition, sanitation, child care, employment income and land. However, such movement towards democratic governance and egalitarian development is being confronted by the neo-liberal economic policies as well as by communal forces.

Communalisation of Behaviour

The colonial establishment sought to create not only a colonial mindset among the people but also inter-religious conflicts. For example, it was wrongly propagated that Indian people are moved uniquely by religious identity and that their social existence is organised around this identity. The colonial regime promoted such divisive communal feelings to weaken the rising tide of anti-imperialist freedom movement. As a result of this continuous divide and rule policy, not only did the Muslim League stay away from the movement but the Hindu Mahasabha and the Rashtriya Swayamsevak Sangh (RSS) also advised their cadre to keep aloof from the movement, at its peak in 1942.[22]

After independence, the communally oriented political forces have continued to use religious identities and related propaganda techniques. As a result, there have been serious communal riots and violence in different parts of the country such as: Mallegan (1967), Ranchi-Hatia (1967), Gorakhpur (1967–69), Gujarat (1969), Bhivandi (1970), Telicherry (1971), Shahdara (1973), Jamshedpur (1979), Meerut (1982), Delhi (1985), Mumbai (1992–93) and Orissa (1999). The state responded to such violence in a set pattern by appointing a 'Commission of Enquiry followed by forgetfulness'.[23]

Efforts at communalising the Indian society which continued inter-mittently were intensified in the late 1980s and early 1990s, culminating in the demolition of the Babri Masjid in December 1992. This communal sacrilege, as could be expected, was followed by widespread riots in the country, most serious of them being in Mumbai.

Reports of the inquiry commissions of the December 1992 and January 1993 riots in Mumbai revealed the intention of the sponsors of the riots to create a permanent divide between the Hindus and the Muslims in order to subjugate the latter to the will of the majority. Rumour-mongering was the most important instrument used to magnify small events, even non-events, to create a dangerous monster. Prior to the riots, organised and orchestrated campaigns of lies and half-truths were undertaken to incite rumours and poison people's minds. So much so that when a victim was torched alive, the crowd was led to clap and dance around his body. The commissions came to the conclusion that the major cause of such heinous crimes was the communal disharmony deliberately created by local thugs and politicians in order to serve their own parochial and self-interests.[24]

People's Needs, Aspirations and Goals of Development: Entrepreneurial Role of the State

People belonging to various Scheduled Castes—Dalits in general—tend now to show significantly greater political assertion as reflected in their changing electoral behaviour. This shows growing resentment against the inborn caste inequality. Such socio-political changes are bound to have an impact on the self-concept of the members of the traditionally marginalised groups. Despite the poor development performance and the negative behaviour of the state, there has been a tremendous expansion of democratic and egalitarian aspirations. Various social legislations, even though not enforced properly, have contributed to increasing self-respect among the traditionally marginalised people which, in turn, has greatly influenced their day-to-day human relationships. They are no longer willing to accept the age-old authority structure. Such psychological changes could trigger off a demand for better quality of life and also for greater democratisation. Development, therefore, needs to be deliberately geared towards the emerging aspirations of the people.

Demand for Better Governance and Performance

The Indian society is thus witnessing two parallel, may be contradictory, processes existing at the same time. The socially conservative forces are trying to communalise society and people's attitudes by inciting religious identities. This is seen clearly in their anti-Christian and anti-conversion movement which is motivated by the fear that the liberation theology could help the Dalits get organised and become assertive. This, in turn would certainly disturb the traditional Hindu society.[25] On the other hand, the age-old deprived sections, the victims of an unequal social order, the Shudras, and the 'outcaste' untouchables are now increasingly asserting, as discussed earlier, for their basic human rights and legitimate place in the country. A strong democratic upsurge among them is reversing the traditional paradigm of electoral democracy, displacing the educated 'ruling' elites as more active participants. Clearly, the implications of such behavioural changes are positive for democracy and social progress. However, it cannot be to the liking of the protagonists of the traditional social order. They are, therefore, using all kinds of propaganda and manipulative techniques to thwart this onward march of democratisation for a more egalitarian and just social order.

One immediate gain of this is that the increased political interest and electoral activism have helped generate a 'demand' for development from below. One of the distinguishing features of the 1999 elections was that there was no one all-India slogan or issue or wave. Instead, local issues, which varied from state to state, made or marred the fortunes of the parties—whether national or regional. Such democratic assessment of the actual governance and performance has the potential of emerging as more powerful than religious and caste appeals.[26] Such increasing democratic concern for better performance has important implications for the functioning of development in the country.

The Duty and Role of the State

The emerging democratic aspirations and increasing assertion of the disadvantaged and the Dalits call for an active role of the state in development. It did occupy the central stage in development theories for several decades after the Second World War. Since the 1980s, its role has, however, come under attack by the anti-interventionist economic theories. These seek to give primacy to market forces via deregulation, budget cuts and privatisation. Contrary to such theories and related policies, it is being increasingly argued, as experience is showing in several countries, that the state has to play an active role in promoting social and economic development of its people. For instance, because of the negative impact of the neo-liberal ideology of minimalist state, Brazil is now giving highest priority to redefining and rebuilding the state. It shares this concern with several other nations from the south and the north alike, including post-socialist Russia, where a void of legitimate state authority has resulted in emergence of mafias instead of efficient *laissez faire*. Similar pathologies (under different names such as privatisation of the state, bureaucratic rings, chrony capitalism) have plagued authoritarian regimes in Latin America, Africa and Asia. Such ideologies have even perverted the model development state in South Korea where crisis was caused by lack of effective regulation and monitoring of the banking system—a default, not excess, of the developmental state.[27]

The miracles of the twentieth century were accomplished against the *laissez faire* and not through it (Hobsbawm, 1994: 563–69). It is well known that the American state played an entrepreneurial role during the period of its catching up in the late nineteenth century. (Kozul-Wright, 1995). Nearer home, soon after independence, India sought to innovate by evolving development strategies of the middle path, giving an active role to the state rooted in its intellectual and political history, at the same time, taking advantage of other countries' experience, both positive and negative (Chakarborty, 1987). Thus, historically, the state, and not the private sector, has played an entrepreneurial role in development.[28]

People's aspirations on the one hand, and the poor development performance in India on the other, calls for an alternative strategy, and new values, attitudes and skills on the part of the development functionaries. This is becoming imperative in view of the changing self-concept of the marginalised people. They are now unlikely to accept dominative and patronising leadership. They are also keen to acquire modern skills and capability and take on an active role, not only in development but also in governance. There is, therefore, a growing pressure on the state to perform, and on the functionaries to adopt more democratic empowering and capability promoting leadership styles.

Though people have an important role to play, the state alone can enforce universal human rights for all. In this sense, civil society cannot be detached from the state. Energisation of civil society, therefore, is very much a part of the democratic state. In recent years, there has been a growing realisation of the usefulness of and faith in the institutions of the state. (Gupta, 1997). It is generally agreed but often forgotten that one of the fundamental conditions of development in East Asia, quoted as a success story, was that the state there played a more autonomous and energetic role than, for instance, in Latin America, where powerful land-owners and private businessmen often prevented land reforms. In fact, the state's role in building capability to enhance the competitiveness of the country was the critical factor in economic growth in East Asia.[29]

Though one of the important messages of the last few electoral verdicts is concern of the people for improving their quality of life and for better governance and development performance, it would not come just, for example, by the introduction of PRIs. It calls for reconceptualisation of development and rethinking about the attitudes and behaviours of the development functionaries in order for them to help promote human rights, obtain individual and collective freedom from the oppressive social system and create greater choice. The state in India has to become more development-oriented in order to shape, pursue and encourage the achievement of explicit goals and objectives.[30] It should feel concerned for preparing and motivating the state functionaries for more effective public services like health care, education, drinking water, public sani-tation, employment generation and a host of other basic needs of the people. The 'demand' from below for better performance, as is now somewhat emerging, should make the state functionaries show greater readiness to learn and effect mid-course corrections in various policies and programmes for obtaining the desired objectives.

Democracy and Development

Collective Imagination: The Role of Civil Society

Political and social movements and emerging competitive electoral politics, as briefly discussed earlier, relate to the wider social context and collective interests and imagination. People have been articulating their desire to see their respective governments work in their interest. They expect the state, in this respect, to play an entrepreneurial and empowering role and the development functionaries to behave accordingly.[31] When the civil society and people's organisations are weak, the dominant elite tends to strengthen centralisation and promote powerlessness in people.[32] However, programmes like agricultural extension, rural development, literacy campaigns and functioning of the PRIs have to necessarily involve people at the ground level.

Instead of promoting such involvement, people can be just incorporated in the development processes. This can take place either by naked clientism or by subtle populism. The former is associated with bosses who provide patronage to people—their clients and recipients. The latter is associated with a charismatic leader who provides patronage, and in another form, by invoking popular dreams[33] as happened so dramatically in the famous Garibi Hatao programme in the early 1970s. Both processes reduce citizens to objects and pawns. Even people's movements can be incorporated into dependency and subordination-oriented politics of the ruling establishment if its members and leaders are not vigilant.[34] Many a times, it is the alternative and subtle, rather than naked patronage which characterises the implementation of our development programmes (Mehta, 1998: 61–66, 73).

Development functionaries, whether political or bureaucratic and/or in non-government development organisations (NGDOs), as social and political activists, have an important role in helping people become catalysts of democratisation. Civil society may not have enough space for such catalyses. The state (including the local bodies and the PRIs) have, therefore, an additional responsibility in preparing and educating people on specific issues and/or around collective interests. However, it has not so far been able to play such a role, as shown by the rampant illiteracy, ill-health and widespread poverty even after more than fifty years of independence, to which the President recently drew our pointed attention.[35] This underlines the important role of people's movements and public activism in energising the state in this direction.[36]

The Practice of Development

The gulf between thought and actual development practice in India is well known. The Preamble and the fundamental rights enshrined in the Indian constitution are confronted by the principle of born inequality. The caste system has been the depository of this inequality. As Radhakrishnan remarked many years ago, 'caste is a source of discord and mischief and if it persists in its present form, it will affect with weakness and falsehood the people that cling to it' (Radhakrishnan, 1940: 378). Such discord is reflected in the negative mutual images of children and adults from different caste and social groups (see Chapter 4). Non-fulfilment of basic needs and growing disparities due to faulty development strategies tend to reinforce such stereotypes and divisive attitudes.

Promoting a Sense of Sameness

It is thus not enough that theories are propounded and promises made to the people. In a democracy, it is up to the state to perform certain duties so that individuals can exercise their rights, without the strong and the privileged always prevailing over the weak. It is not a question of balancing altruism with selfishness because 'persons need one another since it is only in active cooperation with others that one's powers reach fruition. Only in a social union is the individual complete' (Rawls, 1971: 525). All people thus need to have a basic sense of sameness. They need to resemble each other. In a caste-ridden society like ours, it is possible only when it is ensured that the tenet of equality of opportunity is effectively implemented.

The Right to Development

The United Nations has declared that people have the right to development. This right to development also specifies how development has to be implemented—with transparency, accountability, participation of people and equity of access. The World Bank also now tends to draw attention to the urgency of improving governance for meeting the bare and minimum felt needs of the people for 'a public life to be healthy, peaceful and to live and love without hunger.[37] Interestingly, people have been expressing such needs in India for quite some time. Thus, they have been increasingly articulating that, ". . . there is no place to live and there is nothing to eat"; "they have practically no land, no irrigation, not even drinking water, no work in the village or in the neighbourhood, . . . no medical facilities". "Nobody listens to us neither the Minister, nor the Surpanch, nor the Patwari"' (Mehta, 1998: 11–15; also see Mehta, 1995: 130–31).

As seen earlier, the problems of marginalised people have been aggravated by the neo-liberal economic policies being implemented as 'reforms' under the inspiration of the International Monetary Fund (IMF) and the World Bank. Maybe it is due to the negative experience of such 'reforms' that the World Bank is now thinking in terms of the state's role in a Comprehensive Development Framework (CDF). Such a development framework requires strengthening of organisations, the human capacity and structure of the state at various levels. The bank is now stressing the need for moving people 'from powerlessness to democratic culture' . . . 'from weakness to capacity for action' . . . 'Good governance is associated with higher GNP per capita, higher adult literacy and lower infant mortality' . . . 'with weak governance there would be no progress in education, health, water, energy or rural and urban development' there was a need for 'real commitment from each country'. There was a need for training and motivating civil servants and civic leaders to 'improve delivery to the communities they serve'. There was a need to 'create doers of development'.[38]

Such steps by themselves would, however, not change the power structure at the village level.[39] For democratising governance, it is necessary to democratise society. Liberal democracy should, therefore, be more concerned with people rather than things, with their present and future life rather than the legacies from the past. A liberal democratic society should help people from the disprivileged cultures to not only survive but also to move ahead with hope and confidence (Gupta, 1999). In this process, the Constitution of India directs the state to intervene effectively.

Socio-psychological Monitoring: Instrumentation for Interventions

Research in Democratic-Secular Attitudes

The communally oriented political forces, have been seeking to retard the development of resemblances and a sense of sameness by seeking to communalise society. Such forces try various methods in different fields, including education and other such institutions. They spread rumours, distort history, mould curricula and teaching to influence young minds. The teachers' classroom behaviour and their values and attitudes play an important role in this respect. Thus, communalisation and democratisation, as discussed earlier, are underway almost concurrently in the country. The impact of such processes and social learning gets reflected in the attitudes of the people. It would be useful to understand the extent of such attitudes and values for any programme of democratisation and development in the country. Chapters 2 and 3 report research undertaken to evaluate some such psychological dimensions. The study was designed specifically to understand the strength of secular (vs. communal) values and attitudes; social hostility and stereotypes; and democratic (vs. authoritarian) values and attitudes among youth and children. It was assumed that such research instruments would be useful in undertaking social audit, in designing communication strategies and for undertaking training for the promotion of secular-democratic behaviour in children and others.

Research in Development and Work Behaviour

Today, the Indian society, marked by a significant upsurge of Dalit assertion, regional aspirations and keen competitive electoral politics, is characterised by important changes in voting behaviour—with less privileged people showing an enhanced sense of political efficacy and self-esteem and greater interest in democratic institutions than the traditionally efficacious and powerful elite. Development should seek to utilise the changing aspirations of the people and further strengthen their capabilities, to enlarge their choice and enhance freedom. There is a need to divert attention from increasing goods and services to such development of people and their competitiveness. They need to be approached not only as beneficiaries but also as actors. They also now tend to show some concern for better development performance. They want their basic needs fulfilled, equality of opportunities and access to socially-valued goods and services. The values, attitudes and behaviour of the state and other development functionaries, therefore, assume much greater importance at a time when people are becoming more efficacious and conscious.

People's aspirations and the functionaries' work-behaviour thus provide a link between development and democracy (see Chapter 6). In such development, people are encouraged to raise questions and challenge the decisions in a given programme. The programme is sensitive to their aspirations, anguish and anger. It tries to understand not only the manifest content of their communications but also the latent affective tone of their concerns. Development should, therefore, encourage and help them get organised, put forth their demands and protect their interest. Individuals become people when they come together and get organised. Education and organisation of disadvantaged people, therefore, serve an important function of releasing a learning process for democracy.[40]

Studies on democracy have focused mostly on the elite and have shown less interest in popular demands, resistance and organisation. Democracy is not just good governance as the World Bank seems to emphasise (World

Bank 1997). It consists much more of paying attention to the needs and demands of the people. By encouraging organisation and participation, development can greatly help in promoting inter-personal trust among people. Such a trust is important for the formation of social capital—an essential element in making democracy work.[41]

It is the people's learning process which helps the democratic institutions evolve and take roots. Competitive electoral politics has helped people respect and have faith in the democratic institutions. They see them as instruments of realising their age-old dreams. By focusing on the interplay between the 'actors' (the people) and the institutions, development can help deepen civil society (North, 1990). The functionaries have, thus, an important role to play in this connection. Even the World Bank (1997) as mentioned, recognises this in the so-called East Asian miracle and sees the state as a 'facilitator', a 'catalyst' and a 'partner'.

As we know, historical antecedents in India tend to reinforce the inherited colonial and neo-colonial institutions which maintain the hold of the ruling class over the people. This negates and weakens the development process on the ground level to the detriment of the rights of the poor and the vulnerable. This is why the study of civil society is not enough in itself. There is a need to understand the dynamics of dominance, hegemony and dependency. Democratisation requires collectivity of perceptions, imagination and organisation as well as a plan of action that relates to joint interests and visions. In this process of democratisation, actors use democracy for development of choices and freedom. This is an important pre-condition for democracy. Modernity in civil society alone is no guarantee for democracy (see Chapter 4). It can result in an authoritarian modernisation, as happened in the case of Nazi Germany.[42]

Democratisation from below

Because of the entrenched historical antecedents, democratisation in India has to be an anti-feudal struggle also. Development, therefore, has to relate to the people's struggle for their basic rights. Such development is essential for sustaining democracy itself.[43] As we know, authoritarian rule and modernisation may go hand-in-hand. It can create human capital but negate democratisation. The core of human development, therefore, consists of freedom, creation of choices, equal access to opportunities and inculcation of capability and a positive self-concept among the common labouring people. Herein lies the importance of people's movements which evoke collective imagination and enhance their ability to get together for a common interest. This is seen in cases of successful democratic decentralisation in some parts of India which, in turn, has also contributed to agricultural and other development.[44] Thus, there is a significant link between people's movements and development. Sustainable democracy requires democratisation from below with opportunity for people to engage in pro-democratic efforts and to participate, both in the formulation of policies and in their implementation (Migdal, 1994).

Development-related Instruments

The work on the instruments, reported in Chapters 2, 3 and 5, was undertaken in this context of the interface between democracy and development. Such instrumentation was designed to evaluate the ongoing development performance in terms of goals of promoting capability and wider democratisation in the society. The criteria for secular-democratic attitudes and for leadership, problem-solving behaviour and development functioning were set in accordance with such requirements. The items (Chapters 2 and 5; Annexure 1 and Tables 5.1 to 5.4) were informed by the need for an effective interaction between democratisation and development. The instruments also sought to study the sense of self-efficacy, self-esteem and initiative, i.e., the sense of personal efficacy, in the functionaries and managers whether in development and/or at a workplace or an enterprise organisation. Their work-related perceptions were also identified in order to understand their sense of belonging to or sense of alienation from the organisational and developmental goals.

Designing Inputs for Interventions

Another major objective of this research was to prepare instruments which could help in designing interventions, including evaluation, monitoring and training programmes with a view to strengthen secular-democratic attitudes and to motivate development functionaries/managers for the desired empowering, efficacious and capability promoting behaviours. As mentioned before, such values, attitudes and behaviours are necessary for obtaining not only proper and adequate development performance but also for promoting democratisation in the country. Efficacious and democratically-oriented functionaries, whether in government or in non-government organisation, are likely to promote similar values and

psychological empowerment among the people with whom they are supposed to work (see Chapter 7).

Thus, the various instruments (Chapters 2, 3 and 5) were formulated
to undertake related research and to help evaluate the ongoing people's
movements and development programmes with a view to understand
the values, attitudes and behaviours of the various concerned functionaries.
Such socio-psychological monitoring could help in both monitoring
programmes and in undertaking the required corrections for improving
performance. Such monitoring could thus provide a research base for
planning appropriate training programmes and other interventions for
strengthening democratic leadership and capability promoting development behaviours on the ground. Such research and interventions are
likely to help in psychological empowerment of both the functionaries
and the people, thereby contributing to an effective interface between
democracy and development. These could also help strengthen movements and related institutions for strengthening citizenship and actor roles
in people, in turn, contributing to improvement of democratic governance
at all levels. Democratisation (see Chapter 6) is a crucial factor in
functioning of the workplace and other organisations in order to promote
the required capability and competitiveness. It is necessary to note, as
mentioned earlier, that modernity alone is not enough for achieving the
desired goals of development as it could be accompanied by undemocratic
(authoritarian) and non-secular values and attitudes (see Chapter 4). Both
democratisation and development require a secular and harmonious
relationship including inter-personal and inter-group trust. Hence the need
for research and interventions for promoting secular democratic values
and social harmony for achieving equality of opportunity and better access
and other social goals of development. The related research for such
instrumentation and some suggested interventions are reported and discussed in the following chapters.

Notes

1. Such occupational groups, along with others, now form the constitutional categories
   of Scheduled Castes (SCs) and Other Backward Castes (OBCs) in the country.
2. For such tendencies in programme implementation, see Mehta (1998: 42–70) and for
   evidence and discussion of exclusionary communication networks, see Sinha 1999
   and various contributions cited there.
3. For classroom behaviour, see Buch and Santhanam 1970; Mehta 1967/68; Mehta 1969,
   1976a; Mehta and Rao 1973.

4. For a discussion of social implications of such an educational situation and sources of statistics, see Kumar 1998.

5. See 'Satanic Words', in *The Week*, 3 October 1999.

6. The National Commission for Women, therefore, demanded the withdrawal of the book titled '*How to worship Sati*'. The book was a gross violation of the Commission of Sati (Prevention Act), 1997.

7. See Sucheta Dalal, 'Lies, Damned Lies and Market Manipulation', *The Indian Express*, 1 October 1999.

8. *Human Development Report*, Asia 1999, as reported in the editorial, *The Hindustan Times*, 17 September 1999.

9. For discussion of infrastructure, deprivation and quality in education, see Bhatty 1998 and various contributions cited there. For communal exclusiveness among the student youth, see Bhan 1995.

10. For discussion of such mass methods of protest and conservation of environment and for Gandhiji's quote, see Shiva 1989.

11. For movements and social mobilisation, see Sengupta and Roy 1996; Omvedt 1994; Shah 1990; and various contributions in Mohanty et al. 1998. For people's action and social development, see Dreze and Sen (1995: 53, 64, 87–108). Also, see Mehta (1998: 166–67) for some historical factors in Kerala model of social development; and Tornquist et al. 1996 for democratisation.

12. The poor show by the ruling parties in states like Rajasthan, Maharashtra, Orissa, Bihar and Uttar Pradesh in the 1999 elections has been attributed to the poor performance (among other factors) of the incumbent government. See Yogendra Yadav and Sanjeev Kumar (1999) 'Interpreting the Mandate', *Frontline*, 16(25): 120–26.

13. See Gore 1993: 85, for Ambedkar's thoughts on political and social mobilisation of Dalits.

14. See report by Venkitesh Ramakrishnan in *Frontline*, 5 November 1999: 12, 113; Javeed 1999.

15. For a discussion of the changing political scenario, see Yadav 1999.

16. For discussion of political behaviour during the 1960s and 1970s see Mehta 1971b, 1981 and contributions cited there.

17. For some statistics and discussion, see Javeed 1999; see Mehta 1998 for discussion of such structural inhibiting factors in human development.

18. For some statistics, see Pushpendra 1999.

19. For these interesting statistics and discussion, see Javeed 1999.

20. For discussion of such changes in voting behaviour, see Javeed, *ibid*. For discussion of the popular resentment against non-performing governments and the system, see Mehta 1998: 128–32.

21. For discussion of such changes in the tribals including women, mostly illiterate, indicative of psychological modernity and higher aspirations, see Mehta (1995: 163–78).

22. For history of colonial efforts to communalise the Indian society, see Thapar et al. 1977; Chandra 1987.

23. See Rajeev Dhawan, 'The Wadhwa Commission', *The Hindu* (on India server), 5 October 1999.

24. For details of findings and recommendations of the Commissions, see IPHRC 1993; Engineer 1998.

25. For discussion of the issues concerning conversion and the communal politics, see Sarkar 1999.

26. For discussion of the changing electoral appeals, see Yogendra Yadav and Sanjeev Kumar (1999) 'Interpreting the Mandate,' *Frontline*, 16(25): 120–26. Also see *EPW* 1999.

27. For discussion, see Sachs 1998. Also see Deane 1989 for the role of state in economic development.

28. For a discussion of state's entrepreneurial role, see Sachs 1998 and for generating people-oriented entrepreneurship and development, see Mehta (1998: 210–16).

29. For discussion of the role of state in development see, Evans 1987; for competitiveness policy, see Oughton 1997.

30. For a discussion of the model of developmental state, see Leftwich 1995.

31. For discussion of the entrepreneurial role of the state in development, see Ruschmeyer et al. 1992.

32. For discussion and evidence, see Kohli 1987, 1994; Migdal 1994; Mouzelis 1990 and other contributions mentioned there.

33. For discussion of such processes and aspects of democratisation and democracy, see Tornquist (1999: 155–58).

34. For discussion of the processes of appropriation of dissent, see Krishna 1996.

35. Address to the nation by Shri K.R. Narayanan, President of India, on the eve of Republic Day 2000, New Delhi.

36. For discussion of politicisation for democratisation and development, see Tornquist 1999. Also see Mehta (1998: 184–88) for public activism for activising the state.

37. See 'Coalition for Change: Address to the Board of Governors' by James D. Wolfensonn, President, the World Bank, 28 September 1999.

38. *Ibid.*, pp. 6–7.

39. For an insightful story of how the entrenched upper caste leaders use the most backward caste Surpanch (Head) of the village panchayat to transfer funds and resources of the Panchayat for their personal interest, and how they manipulate the constitutional provisions of reservation for the backward castes in governance of the panchayati raj institutions to maintain and preserve their power over village society, see Prabash Joshi 'Benalo Chahe Jitna Kanun, Hoga Kya' (make as many laws, nothing will change) *Jansatta*, 25 December 1999.

40. This learning process of individuals becoming people and a group is observed in training and other programmes for promoting organisation and collective action among the poor. For a report see, Mehta (1995: 120–36).

41. For a discussion on formation of social capital and sustainable development, see Putnam, Robert 1993; Evans 1996.

42. For a discussion of civil society as undergoing a process of secularisation emerging from socio-political churning, see various papers and contributions cited in Alexandar 1998.

43. For discussion of sustainable democracy and democratisation from below, see Przeworski et al. 1995.

44. For discussion of cases of successful democratic decentralisation and development, see Lieten 1996; Thorlind 1998 and for a breakthrough in agriculture and other allied developmental sectors see 'Special Feature: West Bengal', *Frontline*, 14 April 2000: 115–28.

TWO

Measuring Social Prejudices and Democratic-Secular Behaviour: A Report on Instrumentation[1]

Background

Periodic communal clashes and other such emotionally charged situations (see Chapter 1) pose problems to democratisation in the country. Attitudes and behaviour reflected in such conflicts cut at the very roots of our secular, liberal democracy. Some early attempts soon after independence were made to study such conflicts. Mukherjee (1951), Lois Barkley Murphy (1953), Gardner Murphy (1953) and Ram (1955), among others, sought to study various aspects of communal and social tension. Gardner Murphy observed that the hierarchical concept of status in the caste system, supported by the doctrine of Karma, interferes in some ways with the development of an egalitarian spirit in Indian life (1953: 35–36). Lois B. Murphy (1953) traced the roots of prejudice to certain child-rearing practices and childhood experiences, particularly those related to emphasis on dependence rather than independence, early freedom from frustration and lack of opportunities for group planning. Mukherjee (1951) found overt symbolic ways in which caste distance is expressed, compounded by economic factors, to be important in social tension.

Some other studies, such as Devi (1968), George and George (1970), Misra (1962), Sinha and Sinha (1967), drew attention to social stereotypes prevailing in the country. For example, Rath and Sarkar (1960) found two groups belonging to different states tending to agree closely in their description of five target groups. Such studies generally confirmed the well-known fact that there are widely-held stereotypes and prejudices among linguistic, caste and religious groups (see also, Chandra, 1967;

Kuppuswamy, 1962; Shankar, 1966; Sinha and Sinha, 1960; and Sinha and Upadhyaya, 1962). As Kretch et al. (1962) have explained, prejudice is an unfavourable attitude towards an object and tends to be highly stereotyped, emotionally surcharged and difficult to change by contrary information. It may lead to a tendency of avoiding members of the target group. In the Indian context, such communal stereotypes and negative attitudes tend to emotionally surcharge the social ecology of the people.

Preceding and during the period when the present research was undertaken, i.e., during the 1960s and early 1970s, besides empirical studies such as those mentioned earlier, reports by social workers, educationists, journalists and the various riot enquiry commissions provided some useful insights into the communal behaviour. For instance, the Ranchi Riot Enquiry Commission (1967–71) concluded that 'distrust among the major communities and communal attitudes was the main causes of disturbance'. Shah (1970) studied the Ahmedabad riots and found mutual suspicion, feelings of estrangement, lack of sympathy for the victims of the riots, value conflicts, prejudices and widespread rumours as the main sources of conflict. Mehta, Gera and Rao (1974) analysed the content of some 150 such riot-related reports, news items, newspaper articles and despatches with a view to cull out a conceptual model for understanding social and behavioural dimensions of communal conflict. The major psychological causes that emerged were: communal prejudices, mutual mistrust, lack of respect for others and traditional, conservative values and attitudes in certain sections of the population. Certain historical and socio-economic factors and some political parties and communal groups have also been identified as contributing to such psychological predispositions.[2]

The Present Study

The present project was mooted following the Ahmedabad and Bhiwandi riots in 1969–70. It was implemented with three specific purposes, namely, (a) to study and identify some important psychological dimensions of secular behaviour, (b) to identify factors in socialisation and communication processes, that promote 'communal' feelings and attitudes, retard secular behaviour and thereby weaken national integration, and (c) to suggest a communication strategy to combat communalism. The present chapter reports research (conducted in 1969–71) with regard to the first two objectives.

Tools for Data Collection

In pursuance of the first objective mentioned above, it was decided to assemble and/or develop suitable psychological tools for the study. As the communal problem was peculiar to our socio-political scene, it was necessary that the items of the tools were relevant to the experience of the subjects. It was also decided to make the instruments usable as far as possible for both adults as well as children. The instruments thus developed are described below.

Conservative Authoritarian Attitude Scale (CAAS)

It was decided to model the items of CAAS after Adorno's famous work (Adorno et al., 1950). Items were developed for the following dimensions: (a) conservatism (b) authoritarian aggressiveness (c) destructiveness and (d) cynicism. Some previous related research and the then salient national, political, social and constitutional issues were examined and a pool of 40 items, 10 for each dimension, was developed. The subjects were required to respond to each item by marking on a five-point scale from 'strongly agree' to 'strongly disagree'.[3]

Overall Modernity Scale (OM Scale)

The Overall Modernity scale, developed elsewhere (Smith and Inkeles, 1966), was used in the present study. Items of the scale were translated into Hindi and other languages. It contains 13 items and provides a measure of the individual's socio-political modernity.

Secular Attitude Scale (SA Scale)

Several source materials like Sills' International Encyclopaedia of Social Sciences (1968), Seligman's Encyclopaedia of Social Science (1948), literature on national integration some relevant research and the Indian constitution (Pylee, 1965) were searched to develop an original scale on psychological secularity. The following dimensions were kept in mind while developing it:

(a) faith in fundamental rights of the people of India, with particular reference to:

(i) Social Justice, (ii) Liberty, (iii) Equality and (iv) Fraternity;
(b) respect for one's own religion and other religions;
(c) tolerance;
(d) attitude towards material, cultural and social advancement of common people;
(e) patriotism; and
(f) scientific temper with particular reference to:
(i) objectivity, (ii) open-mindedness.

In all, 37 items were prepared and evenly distributed over the above dimensions.[4]

In-group and Out-group Attitude Scales (IGA and OGA Scales)

Scales were developed for the study of inter-communal attitudes as well as attitudes towards one's own community. They were intended to yield information about the extent of communal stereotypes and prejudice among the various sections of the population. Semantic differential scales were considered suitable for this purpose. To begin with, an open-ended questionnaire was prepared to obtain a sample of important prevailing stereotypes. The intention was to obtain information for developing the items for this scale. This questionnaire was administered anonymously and individually to a small group of Hindu and Muslim students and workers in Delhi. The questionnaire contained direct questions which did not find ready response. In a similar second attempt, another questionnaire with indirect questions was administered. These two attempts gave us information about some common stereotypes. In addition to this, some popular Hindi, Gujarati and Marathi short stories and fiction were searched for information about certain common stereotypes. Based on this data and personal experience, a list of suitable adjectives was developed to compose the desired semantic differential scales. The adjectives were bipolar to be rated on a seven-point rating. The scales were modelled after Osgood et al. (1957). To begin with, the inter-communal attitude scale consisted of 38 bipolar adjectives.

Research reviews and documentation (for example, see Hyman, 1959) delineate two separate aspects of authoritarianism. The 'F' Scale (Adorno et al., 1950) gives information on the 'implicit' aspect of political authoritarianism and scales of attitudes provide data on the individual's attitude to civil liberties, equality of sex and, among people particularly, attitude towards minorities. Such scales, therefore, give information on the 'manifest' aspects of authoritarianism. In the present study, it was assumed that the psychological scale on authoritarianism (on the lines of the 'F' scale) would give information about the 'implicit' aspect (or maybe the personality make-up), and the scales on modernity, secularism and communal or social prejudices would provide data on the 'manifest' aspect of authoritarianism. Such instruments together could, therefore, yield information on the implicit (personality) as well as on the 'civic' (manifest) aspects of the secular-communal behaviour.[5]

Standardisation of Tests: Tryout of Instruments

The First Tryout

The first tryout of the instruments was conducted in Delhi. The sample consisted of school and college students, workers, government employees, self-employed artisans, traders and small businessmen belonging to both the major communities—Hindu and Muslim. All data was collected through individual interviews. The authoritarian attitude scale was individually administered to 132 respondents. They responded to each item on a five-point scale ranging from 'strongly agree' to 'strongly disagree'. In some cases the scale was reversed. Similarly, the OM Scale was administered to 116, the SA Scale to 92 and the OGA and IGA Scales to 205 respondents. The interviews were conducted by trained staff of the project. Each interviewer kept a detailed record of experience/ observation concerning wording of items and other aspects of test administration encountered during the fieldwork.

Analysis and Selection of Items

The data thus collected was processed for item analysis. Extreme group method was used for calculating the discrimination power of each item in the various instruments.

CAAS

Twenty (out of 40) items showed good discrimination power. Three of these were dropped as experience showed that these were not well understood by respondents. Similarly, following the field experience, four items, though they did not show good discrimination, were accepted after some rephrasing. These were included in the draft for the second tryout. Variety of situations and dimensions were also kept in mind while selecting items for the second run.

OM Scale

All the items (except one) of the OM scale showed significant discrimination power. Following the field experience, the wording of some items was changed to make them more easily understandable.

SA Scale

Twenty four (out of 37) items showed significant discrimination power. Out of these, four seemed to contain high social desirability. They were dropped. The scale for the second run, thus, contained 20 items.

OGA-IGA Scale

Since these were both in-group as well as out-group attitude scales, item analyses were done for four groups, i.e., Hindus for Hindus, Muslims for Muslims, Hindus for Muslims and Muslims for Hindus. The obtained item discrimination values with respect to each of the four groups were ranked from top-down. Each item thus got four ranks. The items which got a rank of 20 or above in at least three out of four groups were considered for the second run. The interviewer's field experience was also considered while selecting the items. In all 15 items were thus selected.

The Second Tryout

It was decided to conduct the second tryout at some such places as were then affected by communal riots, i.e., just sometime before testing of instruments in 1970–71. The sites thus selected were: Ahmedabad,

Bhivandi and Ranchi. The items, originally developed in Hindi, were translated into Urdu, Marathi and Gujarati. A personal data sheet was prepared and used for the collection of some relevant social background of the respondents.

Training of Interviewers

The data collection was conducted by and/or under the supervision of three staff interviewers, one each at Ahmedabad, Bhivandi and Ranchi. These interviewers and their local helpers were specifically trained for collection of data in view of the sensitive nature of the test material and also that the field work was to be done at some riot-affected sites. Each field interviewer kept a detailed record of his/her impressions/experience with particular reference to problems encountered in getting responses to different items. Such information was later used in revising the tools.

Sampling for the Tryout

The sampling presented a problem because of the complexity of the demographical variables. There was a need to include young students from schools and colleges as well as some other sections of the adult population. The project was located at Delhi and the field work was to be done at far-off places. The census data of 1961 showed that the major constituents of the population in the three towns were government employees, businessmen, shopkeepers, industrial workers, trade and commerce workers, self-employed artisans and some others. It was decided to draw respondents from all these major categories of the local population. The sample thus became more purposive rather than representative. As the data collection was to be done individually, it was decided to draw about 100 persons randomly as far as possible at each site, half of whom were students. Further, they were equally divided between riot-affected and peaceful areas of the town. As per the sampling needs and the design and the prior information thus collected, the interviewers went and interviewed a few persons of a given occupational category in each of the selected areas. Such respondents then composed the non-student sample. During the time of data collection, the schools and colleges were closed. The students were, therefore, interviewed at a few of the lodges and hostels. Thus, some 157 students and about 150 non-students were,

Table 2.1
Composition of the Sample Included in the Second Field Tryout

Place	Area	Students				Employees		Businessmen and Shopkeepers		Industrial Workers		Other Trade Workers		Total
		College		School										
		H	M	H	M	H	M	H	M	H	M	H	M	
Ahmedabad	Riot affected	13	3	10	22	5	4	5	4	1	3	3	6	84
	Peaceful	4	2	3	–	1	3	–	–	–	2	–	2	22
	Total	17	5	13	22	6	7	5	4	1	5	3	8	104
Ranchi	Riot affected	–	–	–	12	3	4	3	5	5	5	–	–	55
	Peaceful	13	12	13	–	2	2	2	3	3	4	–	1	45
	Total	13	12	13	12	5	6	5	8	8	9	–	–	100
Bhivandi	Riot affected	13	12	–	12	3	2	5	3	2	5	3	3	81
	Peaceful	–	–	13	–	1	2	2	2	2	2	2	2	20
	Total	13	12	13	12	4	4	7	5	4	7	5	5	101
Grand Total		**43**	**29**	**39**	**46**	**15**	**17**	**15**	**17**	**13**	**21**	**8**	**13**	**305**

Notes: H = Hindus; M = Muslims.

interviewed for the second tryout of the instruments. The breakdown of the tryout sample is shown in Table 2.1.

Item Analysis: Criteria for Selection of Items

The tools were developed, as mentioned before, concurrently in Hindi, Urdu, Gujarati and Marathi. Separate analyses were carried out for the various instruments for each language group. The extreme group method was used to study the internal consistency of each item within the given instrument.

The analysis thus yielded three discrimination values (one each for three language groups) for each item. The first criterion for selection of the given item was that it showed significant discrimination in at least two out of three groups. The field report on understandability and acceptability of the given item was also considered. The items thus selected were processed for factor analysis with a view to identify clusters so that suitable scales could be carved out. Some items were further weeded out in this process. The results of factor analysis are discussed later in the chapter.

CAA Scale

Following the given criteria, all the items in the CAAS showed significant discrimination in, at least, two out of three groups. However, item 9 ('strikes impede the country's progress') was dropped as the field report showed that many respondents did not follow it. Similarly, it was reported that another item (religion must increase its influence in nation's life) was not followed by many semi-literate adults. Thus, 18 items were finally selected to compose the conservative authoritarian attitude scale (CAAS).

OM Scale

Twelve out of 13 items showed acceptable discrimination power. One item did not do well as its DP values for Gujarati and Hindi versions were not significant. As the scale was an adapted version of the original scale, it was decided to keep it intact, retaining all the items. Some minor language changes were, however, made in some items in all the three language versions in order to make them more understandable.

SA Scale

Two of the 20 items did not show the acceptable discrimination power. One was dropped on the basis of field interviewers' report. The remaining 17 items were selected and processed for factor analysis following which, four more items were dropped.

IGA–OGA Scales

The same pairs of adjectives were used for the study of inter-group as well intra-group images. These were, however, treated as separate scales for the purpose of item analysis. All the 15 items showed good discrimination power for all the three languages, both for in-group and out-group images. However, the field reports showed that the list was rather long and did not find favour with the respondents. As the purpose of the scales was to study in-group and out-group stereotypes, only the most evaluative items were retained. Ten adjectives which showed substantially high loading on the first factor, as seen in Appendix 4, were finally selected to compose these scales to measure social prejudice.[6]

Instrument Validity and Reliability

Items in the various instruments were assembled, as mentioned before, on certain theoretical assumptions. The analysed and selected items were processed through factor analysis to test the validity of the constructs and also, to identify item clusters to compose sub-scales in each instrument. The data was run for centroid factors. Only such factors which showed an eigen value of 0.08 or more were rotated by the varimax method through five iterations. Each instrument was analysed separately. Thus, five factors emerged in the Conservative Authoritarian Attitude scale (CAAS); three in the OM; five in the Secular Attitude scale (SAS); and two in the In-group–Out-group Attitude (IGA–OGA) scales.

Several items showed significant loadings on more than one factor. Only a few items showed significant loadings on Factors 3 and 4 of CAAS. For the purpose of scale construction, such items were included under another factor on which they showed low, but significant, loadings. Some items were dropped as these showed no significant loading on any factor. Thus, three sub-scales emerged in CAAS, two in OMS, two in SAS and one in IGA-OGA scales. These factors were labelled respectively as: religious dogmatism, misanthropism and conservative moralism (in CAAS); openness and general awareness (in OMS); tolerance and mutual trust and equalitarianism in SAS; and social hostility in OGAS (for statements along with their loadings, see Appendix 1: Appendices 1 to 4).

The factors mentioned here, along with related items, formed sub-scales of the respective instruments. Thus: the sub-scales of religious dogmatism showed 40 per cent, conservative moralism 38 per cent and misanthropism 22 per cent, of the total variance in the CAA scale. Openness and general awareness respectively, showed 65 per cent and 35 per cent of the total variance in the OM scale and the two sub-scales in the SA scales, i.e., tolerance and mutual trust and equalitarianism respectively showed 49 per cent and 51 per cent of the total variance.

Cross-validity of the Constructs and the Instruments

The item analysis provided an index of internal consistency of the respective instrument. The various tests were developed to help identify some psychological correlates of secular-communal behaviour. It was postulated, theoretically, that the various variables will be intercorrelated in certain ways—some negatively, some positively. The obtained inter-test correlations are seen in Table 2.2. It shows some interesting findings.

Table 2.2
Intercorrelation Matrix (N = 269)

Scales	VAR	1	2	3	4	5
CAA scale	1	–	−0.26**	−0.28**	0.22	−0.12*
OM scale	2	–	–	0.31**	−0.004	0.13*
SA scale	3	–	–	–	−0.18**	0.17**
OGA scale	4	–	–	–	–	0.11
IGA scale	5	–	–	–	–	–

Notes: *Significant at 0.05 level.
　　　　**Significant at 0.01 level.

Thus, the greater the authoritarianism, the lower was the psychological modernity and secularism. Such a person tended to be hostile not only to the out-group (i.e., in this case, Hindu for Muslim and vice-versa) but he also did not have a positive image of his own group. These findings confirmed that the lower the faith in people and the greater the conservative moralistic tendency, the lower was the sense of openness, mutual trust and equalitarianism and also, general awareness. Interestingly, Adorno et al. (1950) also reported that as freedom from religious dogmas goes with 'liberalism', it reduces social prejudice. On the other hand, religiosity, distrust and conservatism are the correlates of authoritarianism. Further, the present study showed insightful cross-validity of the given constructs. For instance, religious dogmatism, misanthropism and conservative moralism (factors in authoritarianism) were negatively correlated with factors of openness and general awareness (in modernity) and also, with tolerance, mutual trust and equalitarianism (the factors in SA scale). Theoretically, the instruments, therefore, showed high validity and worked well in the predicted direction.[7]

The OM and the SA scales showed positive and significant but low intercorrelation. This showed that the two scales have some overlap as well as certain distinctive features. Theoretically also, there is some overlap between the factors of openness (in modernity) and tolerance and mutual trust (in secularity). However, factors like equalitarianism and general awareness are distinct as well as alike. Along with such positive overlap, these two scales served two distinct functions. This was shown by the nature of their correlation with out-group hostility. The SA scale showed a low but significant negative correlation whereas the OM scale did not show any correlation with it (the OGA scale). Thus, a secular person tended to show less inter-group hostility while, a psychologically modern person was necessarily not less inter-group hostile. The factor analysis also suggested the possibility of such relationships. While general awareness could coexist with out-group hostility, a tolerant, trustful, equalitarian person was less likely to show out-group hostility and prejudices.[8]

Interestingly, there was a significant positive correlation between modernity and social prejudice. It suggested, for example, that programmes like those designed to promote family planning (involving psychological modernity) and adoption of such modern practices (see Appendix 2) may not necessarily lead to reduction of social prejudice. McClelland (1969) even found a positive correlation between traditionalism and entrepreneurial behaviour, 'modernity' seems to relate to life situations which tend to promote a sense of alienation. This was confirmed by Singh (1971) who found a positive correlation between alienation and modernity. Thus, sense of alienation was not indicative of lack of modernity. Such findings got support from the obtained positive correlation (see Table 2.2) between modernity and social prejudice and hostility. For further discussion, see Chapter 4.

The psychological factors identified in the SA scale were similar to behaviours identified in some case studies conducted in the riot-affected areas of the country. For instance, Prasad (1953) found a strong sense of identification with one's own community and/or caste, accompanied by perception of the other community as alien. This factor was the main cause of tension. Murphy (1953) also observed that religious dogmas, mutual distrust, intolerance and conservatism interfered with the development of an egalitarian spirit in Indian life. Comparison of OM factors with findings elsewhere yielded interesting similarities. For example, the two identified factors or sub-scales of the OM scale were similar to Schnaiberg's (1970: 411) indicators of modernity in Turkish students. Kahl (1968) also obtained similar factors in his Mexican and Brazilian samples. As mentioned earlier, the CAA scales were developed on the lines of the authoritarian personality (Adorno et al., 1950). Although the basic underlying theoretical assumptions were the same, the items were formulated with particular reference to revivalist communal conservatism and to the desired national goals of secular and democratic society.[9]

Thus, the results of factor analysis and the nature of inter-test correlations showed good theoretical cross-validity of the various tests developed to identify psychological factors in implicit as well as in manifest authoritarianism and in secularism, modernity and social prejudice.

Test Reliability

The maximum obtainable score in each scale was used as N (the number of items in the test) in calculating K-R-21 reliability. The results are seen in Table 2.3. Except the OM scale, the obtained reliability results for the various instruments were quite good. The reliability for the various instruments found in a subsequent study are reported in Chapter 3.

Table 2.3
Reliability of the Scales (N = 304)

Scale	K-R-21 Reliability
1. CAA scale	0.71
2. OM scale	0.48
3. SA scale	0.68
4. IGA scale	0.84
5. OGA scale	0.80

Thus, all the instruments showed good item discrimination, item consistency and homogeneity. The instruments also showed good reliability and theoretical and cross-validity. These were, therefore, reliable tests of measuring and understanding some important psychological and ideological correlates of authoritarian and communal behaviour. The next chapter reports on the applicability of these instruments to school children. Some factors in home and school socialisation as correlates of such behaviours are discussed in Chapter 4.

Notes

1. Fieldwork for the research reported in this chapter was done in 1969–71. Some time later, a brief paper based on that research was published (Rao and Mehta 1978). The present chapter gives details of various instruments developed for this project. Citation of related research studies and other documents pertain to the period preceding the present research then undertaken. The review of research has not been updated in order to maintain the historicity and timing of the study.

2. For some other research on social tension and stereotypes in India, and on the role of history and politics, see Ghurye (1968: 113–99). For socialisation by political parties, see Coleman (1965: 18–25). For analysis of mass violence, see Wells 1972; in India, see Ganguli 1972, and for social prejudice and role of mass media in spreading stereotypes, see Kanta 1953.

3. Adorno et al. 1950 have emphasised the following dimensions of authoritarianism: power and toughness—to admiring power and strength. On this basis, it is hypothesised that authoritarian individuals are more attracted to powerful persons—both in real life and in fantasy; cynicism—the authoritarian individual is inherently cynical about other human beings and characterised by 'contempt for mankind' (p. 239); superstition—they are highly superstitious and believe in 'mystical or fantastic external determinants of the individuals' fate' (p. 236); submission—the authors emphasise the tendency of a prejudiced person to maintain a 'submissive, uncritical attitude toward idealised moral authorities of the in-group (p. 255)'; intraception—the authoritarian individual is opposed to intraception and particularly to psychotherapy and psychiatry, presumably because he is 'afraid of what might be revealed if he, or she thus, should look closely at himself' (p. 235); aggression—the authoritarian persons wishes to condemn, reject and punish those who violate in-group values (p. 232); sex—they are particularly impressed by the 'concern with overt sexuality' (p. 240) which characterises authoritarian individuals and their willingness to severely punish violation of sexual norms.

4. See Almond and Verba 1963 for some secular dimensions of civic culture pp.1–36. See also Kothari (1970: 227–29) for discussion of political culture and the emergence of secular ideology.

5. See Hyman 1959. He says that the 'F' scale contains little in the strict ideological sense that would constitute manifestation of fascism, anti-democratic or endorsement of political authoritarianism. Instead, it contains items which measure such processes as 'projectivity', 'superstition and stereotype', 'anti-intraception', 'sex', 'destructiveness and cynicism', etc. The connections between these levels of personality and political behaviour may be posited on the basis of an elaborate theory or demonstrated through empirical methods (p. 30).

6. Details of item analyses of data are in Mehta 1975a.

7. Similar results have been reported elsewhere. For detailed critical review of such inter-relationship among the psychological variable, see Christie and Jahoda 1966. See also Bhusan 1967; Mohanty and Singh 1966. Also see Adorno et al. (1950: 162–70).

8. Such interesting relationship between secularity and modernity has been widely reported. See Gautam 1970; Gusfield 1967; Hommond 1966; and Inkeles and Singh 1968.

9. See Kothari 1970 for a discussion of political culture and its secular dimensions.

THREE

Measuring Democratic-Secular Attitudes in School Children[1]

A child is not born communal. He learns and acquires communal or secular attitudes and other related behaviours in life, maybe early in life. A review of research showed that most reports and/or studies were conducted and/or focused on college students and/or adults (See Chapter 2; also see Ranchi Enquiry Commission Report, 1967 and Shah, 1970). It is widely believed that education contributes to the development of individual modernity. For example, Inkeles and Smith (1974: 135–43) found correlation of 0.71 between the two, i.e., between education and modernity. In cross-cultural studies, including one in India, such findings suggested that there were other psychological factors which motivated communal behaviour in educated people in spite of their being 'modern'. Our own research, (see Chapter 2), showed that a 'modern' person was not necessarily more tolerant and less inter-group hostile. Such findings showed the need for understanding the sources of learning of attitudes and values early in life, which contributed to social prejudice, therefore, retarding inculcation of democratic and secular behaviour.

Secular and Democratic Behaviour in School Children

Standardisation of Instruments

The present study was conducted to identify some aspects of the secular-communal behaviour in children and to understand some of the sources of such learning and socialisation. The instruments were originally developed on samples of adults. However, while processing the items of the various instruments (see Chapter 2), care was taken to see that they were also usable for children. It was decided to check empirically to see whether these were really applicable to children. This chapter reports the research undertaken in this respect. We then report and discuss some substantive issues in relation to the sources of socialisation in Chapter 4.

One important purpose of the study was to locate factors in the socialisation processes of children which retarded democratic-secular attitudes and instead tended to foster communal social ideology and attitudes. It was assumed, in this connection, that the nature of school management plays an important role in releasing socialisation processes at school. Thus, a communally oriented school management could contribute to creating conditions for children to imbibe communal attitudes. The home environment also is known to be important in the socialisation of children. For purposes of the present study and for the sake of sampling, it was assumed that caste Hindu and Muslim homes provided different kinds of environment than that provided by Scheduled Tribe (ST) and Scheduled Caste (SC) homes. Following such an assumption, five schools were selected purposively. Among these, two were government and three private-aided schools in Udaipur city of Rajasthan. The management of the three private-aided schools was known to be parochial and oriented towards either 'Hindu' or 'Muslim' 'communal' ideology. These schools were located in areas predominantly inhabited by the respective communities. The two government schools were located on the outskirts of the town, somewhat segregated from the mainstream of city life—one at the west-end of the city near a SC colony and the other near a mixed, lower middle class and workers' locality. Most of the children in the five selected schools belonged to the lower and middle social class except a few who came from the upper middle class.

A purposive stratified sample of 190 children, from 5th to 8th grades, was drawn from the five schools as seen in Table 3.1. As the table shows, almost all the SC and ST children were enrolled in the government-managed schools and the large majority of the caste Hindu and Muslim children in the parochially-managed private schools.

Table 3.1
Distribution of the Sample

School	Caste/Community				Total
	Hindu	*Muslim*	*SC*	*ST*	
Government managed	14	7	32	41	94
'Hindu' managed	40	2	3	3	48
'Muslim' managed	2	43	1	2	48
Total	**56**	**52**	**36**	**46**	**190**

Applicability of the Instruments

The same instruments as developed for the study of adults as mentioned earlier, were used in the present study. However, for checking their applicability, a tryout was conducted on some pupils of classes 5, 6, 7 and 8 in three schools similar to those included in the sample. The instruments were administered individually to each child with a view to finding out whether she/he followed the meaning of the items. Most children of class 5 could not follow the items. Some older children found difficulty with Urdu as well as Hindi versions of the terms. Some language changes were, therefore, made in a few items without changing the meaning. Thereafter, the instruments were administered to children in the five chosen schools. The tests were given as a part of the routine class activity in two sittings separated by an interval of one week. There were only a few girls, who were later dropped from the study and 190 boys were retained for the analyses. It was decided to repeat some of the analyses so as to find out their sustainability, reliability and validity for the school children.

Item Analysis

An item analysis of the various instruments showed their good discrimination values. All the 't' values, except one in the CAA scale, were highly significant. In fact, the results showed that the discrimination values were appreciably higher in the case of children as compared to those obtained for the adults. The most discriminating items were those dealing with: supernatural power, family planning and inter-personal relations in the CAA scale; mass media, scientific approach and concern for national problems in the OM scale; and equal rights, protection of life and property and equal opportunities for women in the SA scale.[2]

Reliability

Tables 3.2 and 3.3 give KR_{20} and the split-half reliability values for the scales. If anything, the results obtained here were slightly higher, except in the case of the SA scale, than those obtained on a mixed group of adults, as reported in Chapter 2. The present version of the OM scale showed improved reliability here than the original reliability of 0.716 as reported by Smith and Inkeles (1966). The reliability indices for the sub-scales, though highly significant, were somewhat lower than the respective total instrument.

Table 3.2
Reliability of Total Scales **(N = 190)**

Scale	KR_{20}	Split-Half
CAA scale	0.719	0.823
OM scale	0.629	0.750
SA scale	0.602	0.675
IGA scale	0.733	0.811
OGA scale	0.693	0.765

Table 3.3
Reliability of Sub-scales **(N = 190)**

Sub-scales	KR_{20}	Split-Half
Religious dogmatism	0.593	0.629
Conservative moralism	0.583	0.643
Misanthropism	0.631	0.682
Openness	0.563	0.653
General awareness	0.621	0.593
Tolerance and mutual trust	0.653	0.673
Equalitarianism	0.629	0.708
Social hostility	0.601	0.678

Validity

The obtained inter-correlations, as seen in Tables 3.4 and 3.5, confirmed the theoretical assumptions. Religious dogmatism, on the one hand, showed significant positive correlations with conservative moralism, misanthropism and social hostility and on the other, negative correlations with openness, general awareness, tolerance and mutual trust, and equalitarianism. Theoretically, it thus appeared that a child, high on religious dogmas, also showed greater moralism, misanthropism and social hostility. On the other hand, such a child seemed to be less tolerant and trustful and less equalitarian in his behaviour. All the three sub-scales of the CAA scale showed highly significant positive inter-correlations indicating internal homogeneity of the constructs contained in the total scale. Both conservative moralism and misanthropism showed significant negative correlations with the sub-scales of the OM and the SA scales. It was an important finding which showed the link between implicit and explicit authoritarianism.[3] The openness scale showed significant positive correlations with general awareness, tolerance and mutual trust and equalitarianism, and negative non-significant correlations with social hostility. Thus, a more open person seemed to show greater general awareness, mutual trust and equalitarianism and a low sense of social hostility. General awareness also showed significant positive correlations with the sub-scales of the SA scale (tolerance and mutual trust and equalitarianism). Interestingly, it (general awareness) showed significant positive correlation with social hostility. It showed that a generally informed person could also be high on out-group hostility. On the other hand, the five sub-scales of the CAA and SA scales seemed to be good predictors of social prejudice. These were remarkable findings which showed that children with authoritarian tendency showed greater out-group hostility than those with greater belief in secularism.

The sub-scales of the OM and the SA scales showed significant positive correlations among themselves. This suggested an overlap of constructs in these scales. However, despite this overlap, the two scales (OM and SA) served distinct purposes. This was shown by the fact that openness, a sub-scale of OMS, showed practically no correlation with social hostility, whereas tolerance and mutual trust and equalitarianism, the two sub-scales of SAS, showed significant negative correlations with social hostility. Such findings assumed greater importance as these were similar to those obtained on adults (see Table 3.2). Furthermore, the CAA, OM and the SA scales showed significant positive correlations with in-group image. It was interesting that while the children high on 'modernity' and 'secularism' also tended to evaluate their 'in-group' positively, the 'authoritarian' child did so highly positively.[4] The findings were significant from the point of education and socialisation. For achieving greater social cohesion and harmony, it was not enough to inculcate modernity in children. What was more important was to educate them to imbibe tolerance, mutual trust and a spirit of equalitarianism.

Table 3.4

Intercorrelation Matrix: Sub-scales

	VAR	1	2	3	4	5	6	7	8
1 Religious dogmatism	1	–	0.372	0.293	–0.266	–0.307	–0.205	–0.319	0.352
2 Conservative moralism	2			0.282	–0.321	–0.283	–0.218	–0.197	–0.261
3 Misanthropism	3				–0.363	–0.244	–0.353	–0.223	0.432
4 Openness	4					0.256	0.243	0.319	–0.108*
5 General awareness	5						0.189	0.213	0.201
6 Tolerance & mutual trust	6							0.293	–0.326
7 Equalitarianism	7								–0.286
8 Social hostility	8								–

Notes: *All are significant at 0.01 level except this one, which was not significant.

Table 3.5
Intercorrelation Matrix: Scales **(N = 190)**

Scales	VAR	1	2	3	4	5
CAA scale	1	–	–0.23**	–0.19*	0.31**	0.17**
OM scale	2		–	0.16*	0.15*	0.12
SA scale	3			–	0.16*	–0.24**
IGA scale[†]	4				–	0.17*
OGA scale	5					–

Notes: *Significant at 0.05 level.
   **Significant at 0.01 level.
   † Scoring reversed to show positive direction.

The Working of the Instruments with Children

The findings showed that all the instruments worked well with school pupils. These contained good item discrimination power and showed satisfactory item validity, test and sub-scale reliability, and good theoretical validity. All obtained results, except one, were in the same direction as those obtained from the mixed adult group in the study reported in Chapter 2. The 'authoritarian' children, in contrast to 'authoritarian' adults, tended to evaluate their in-group positively. In the case of adults, the CAA scale showed negative correlation with in-group attitude whereas it was positive in the case of children. Maybe, the 'authoritarian' children were still innocent and more friendly with their in-group, peers.[5] It was, however, remarkable that all the sub-scales and the instruments worked so well with school children. These instruments were then used to study the sources and nature of social learning of such attitudes and values in children. The findings are reported and discussed in Chapter 4.

Notes

1. This chapter is based on research undertaken in 1972–73. Most of the contributions cited in the chapter also relate to that period. These have not been updated in order to maintain the given historical perspective in which the research was then conducted. The full report on this research is available in manuscript form (see Mehta 1975a).
2. Details of item analysis, such as item mean scores, discrimination power and the items in the various instruments, are available in the original report (See *ibid.*).
3. See Hyman (1959: 29–34). He presents data showing the link between implicit and manifest authoritarianism.

4. See Gusfield 1967 for a discussion on tradition and modernity, and its differences with secularism; and also, Portes 1973.
5. Also see Adorno (1950: 551–55, 796, 813); and Seigal 1956, for such implicit and explicit behaviour.

Socio-political Attitudes in Children: Source of Socialisation and Learning[1]

The Home: Parental Socialisation

The influence of social class on parental as well as children's values and attitudes is well known.[2] One of the main objectives of the present study, as mentioned in Chapter 3, was to identify sources of such social learning in children. One such factor could be the fathers' social class which could influence children's attitudes, as implied and/or manifested in authoritarian conservatism, secular attitudes, modernity and social prejudice. The social class is a multi-dimensional concept. Generally, education, occupational position and income have been used to derive an index of an individual's social class or socio-economic status (SES). The educational level and occupational position generally show high positive inter-correlations.[3] In an American study, Hollingshead and Fredrick (1958) found occupation and education as significant predictors of values, with the latter as more important.

In the present study, the father's social class was used as an index of the child's home environment. It was assumed that the more educated and lowly-educated fathers were likely to shape and provide different kinds of home environments to their children. Such differences could be due to their different values. In view of the relationship found between social class and parental values and also because of practical limitations of the present project, it was decided to use the fathers' educational level as an index of their social class and also of the home environment of the children under study. The father's occupation was also used to check on the obtained findings later in some secondary analyses.

Children's Attitudes by Social Groups

School children were classified into four social groups on the basis of their fathers' educational level as seen in Table 4.1. These four groups of children, irrespective of their school, were then studied for authoritarianism, secular values and attitudes, modernity, in-group (self) image and out-group image (social distance and prejudice).

Table 4.1
Fathers' Educational Level and Social Class

	Fathers' Educational Level			
	No Education	*Some Education*	*Secondary Education*	*College Education*
Social group	1	2	3	4
Number of cases	29	76	66	19

Authoritarianism

The children showed differences on authoritarianism (vs. democratism) by their fathers' educational level as seen in Figure 4.1. The children of more educated fathers showed significantly less authoritarian behaviour than those of less educated fathers ($F = 2.86$; $p < 0.05$). The children of fathers with no education and those with some education showed no difference in this respect ($t = 0.21$; NS). Similarly, the children of secondary educated fathers and of those with higher education also showed no difference in this respect ($t = 0.83$; NS). Thus, these two groups of children, i.e., those of fathers with no or some education and those of fathers with secondary and higher education, showed significant differences in their attitudes. The findings here were similar to some other well-known findings in this regard.[4]

Secularism (vs. Communalism)

These findings regarding authoritarianism (vs. democratism) were confirmed by the trends in children's attitude to secularism (vs. communalism). The same two groups of children as mentioned earlier, showed significant difference in this respect ($F = 2.91$; $p < 0.05$). Also, children of fathers with no education and those with some education showed no difference ($t = 0.32$; NS). The same was the case with the children of secondary educated and those of higher educated fathers ($t = 1.67$; NS). Thus, the fathers' education was found to be a significant factor in the attitude

Figure 4.1
Children's Attitudes by Father's Educational Level

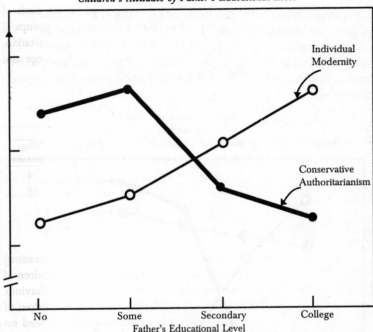

of secularism in children. The difference, however, was visible only in cases where fathers were sufficiently educated, at least upto the secondary level. Here also, the results were similar to some well-known findings in this regard. (Hyman, 1959: 29–34).

Psychological Modernity in Children

The fathers' educational level also emerged as a significant factor in children's psychological modernity (F = 13.39; p < 0.05). In fact, as seen in Figure 4.1, fathers' education showed a linear positive relationship with children's psychological modernity. There were differences between children of fathers with no education and those with some education as well as between children in the two higher groups (all 't' values were significant). The movement of fathers from no education to some education thus seemed to make a significant difference in their children's individual modernity. Here again, the findings confirmed some well-documented research in this regard.[5]

In-group (self) Image

Interestingly, fathers' education made no difference in the children's image of their own community group ($F = 1.64$; NS). The self-group image was uniformly positive as seen in Figure 4.2. All children, irrespective of their fathers' education, thought that their community group was kind, reliable, honest, patriotic and fair. They all showed equally positive stereotypes in this respect.[6]

Figure 4.2
Children's Self-image and Social Attitudes by Father's Educational Level

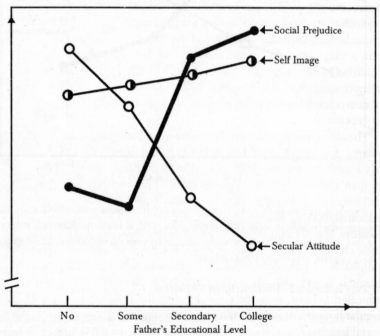

Out-group Hostility in Children

The image of the out-group was just the reverse of the self (in-group) image, as seen in Figure 4.2. Fathers' education once again appeared as a significant factor in children's attitudes towards the out-group ($F = 2.81$; $p < 0.05$). Similar to other findings, children in the first two categories of fathers' education as well as those in the remaining two categories did not show any difference in such hostile social attitudes. On the other hand, children of fathers with no or some education showed significantly greater out-group hostility than those of fathers with secondary or higher education. Social prejudices in children, therefore, seemed to get weakened with increasing fathers' education. Here also, the results confirmed some other well-known findings in this regard.[7]

The Influence of Home in Learning of Social Attitudes

The above findings clearly showed the importance of fathers' education in social learning of children. Educated fathers tended to promote democratic-liberalism (as against authoritarian communalism), psychological modernity and also inter-group harmony (as opposite of inter-group hostility) in children. In view of rampant illiteracy in the country, it was a very significant social finding that fathers' lack of education contributed significantly to the learning of both implicit and manifest authoritarianism in their children. There were far-reaching implications of such relationships for social progress, democratisation and development in the country.

The above findings also implied differential parental values and child-rearing practices. Brofenbrénner (1958) found the middle class parents to be more 'permissive' and the working class parents more 'restrictive' in their child-rearing. Himmelweit (1957) found similar differences in child-rearing practices in the U.K. Kohn (1966) found that the lowly educated working class parents tended to inculcate values reflecting conformism and the middle class parents values reflecting self-direction in their children.[8] Thus, fathers' social class, more particularly their educational level, has been repeatedly found to be a factor in their own, i.e., parental as well as in their children's values. It seemed that the lowly educated fathers promoted parochial and the better educated fathers secular home environment with corresponding implication for children's social learning.[9]

The School: Impact on
Children's Attitudes and Personality

Besides home, school is another important source of children's socialisation. They learn socio-political values and attitudes through interaction with peers, teachers and others, and by their participation in various curricular and co-curricular activities. School influence on socialisation of children has been well documented.[10] As mentioned in Chapter 3, the main objective here was to study the influence of informal school environment (rather than formal teaching, etc.) on children's attitudes. Five schools were selected for the study. Of these, two were government-managed schools which catered predominantly to SC and ST children. The remaining three schools were parochially-managed private schools—one of them, by pronouncedly 'Hindu', and the other two by pronouncedly 'Muslim', community-oriented management committees. These schools were founded and were being run by people known for their parochially-oriented thinking and activities. It was, therefore, assumed in the present project that such parochially-oriented 'managements' were likely to promote a less secular and more parochial/communal school environment. This, in turn, was likely to promote/reinforce corresponding social learning in children. It was further assumed, in this case, that the government-managed schools were likely to provide a more secular environment to their children, with corresponding implications for their social learning.

Psychological Modernity: In-group Image

The children did not show any significant inter-school difference on psychological modernity and also in their self-evaluation, i.e., in the image of their own community group (see Table 4.2). The finding suggested that such psychological modernity was more a function of formal teaching rather than of the informal school environment. The schools were teaching the same courses and curriculum. In fact, some studies have reported a gain of 1.8 points on the OM scale for every additional year of schooling.[11]

Table 4.2
Mean Scores on Psychological Dimensions by School Management

Psychological Dimensions	Schools			F	P
	Government Managed	Privately Managed (Hindu)	Privately Managed (Muslim)		
Modernity	21.7	20.9	18.9	2.38	NS
In-group image	17.3	15.7	16.6	2.83	NS
Secularism	26.8	23.8	24.5	5.29	0.01
Authoritarianism	52.9	56.5	55.3	3.75	0.05
Social prejudice	51.3	56.7	55.6	4.72	0.01
Number of cases	94	48	48		

Psychological Secularity: Secularism

Children in the government schools showed significantly greater secular thoughts and attitudes (see Table 4.2) than those in the parochially-managed schools. While there was no difference between the parochial schools themselves in this respect, the children of both these schools showed lower secular tendency or greater communal tendency than those in the government schools. This was in striking contrast to the finding regarding individual modernity. This suggested that the learning of secular-communal thoughts and attitudes was more a function of 'informal' education and the general environment in the schools. The assumption made regarding the importance of the 'nature of school management' was confirmed. It was found to make a significant difference in the social learning of children. This could have been due to the general school ethos created by informal education, co-curricular and extra-curricular activities and similar other methods.

Authoritarianism

The school 'management' also appeared as a significant factor in authoritarianism among children, as seen in Table 4.2. Here also, the 'Hindu' and 'Muslim' school children did not show significant difference ($t = 0.37$; NS). The government school children, on the other hand, showed significantly lower authoritarianism (or greater democratism) than those in the 'Hindu' ($t = 2.11$; $p < 0.05$) and 'Muslim' ($t = 1.97$; $p < 0.05$) parochially-managed schools.

Social Prejudice

The school 'management' also emerged as a significant factor in children's social prejudice. Children in both 'Hindu' and 'Muslim' schools showed significantly (both $p < 0.01$) greater social prejudice than those in the government-managed schools. The former showed no difference between themselves.

Communalisation of Children's Attitudes

The results showed that the parochially-oriented private school management was a significant factor in communalisation of children's attitudes and values. Those studying in such privately-managed schools (as compared with those in government schools) consistently showed greater authoritarianism (i.e., religious dogmatism, misanthropism and conservative moralism), lower secularism (mutual trust and tolerance, and equalitarian rationalism) and greater social distance with 'other' community groups. That such children tended to show uniformly negative image of other groups indicated that hostile 'out-group' images were formed in rather early age (see Figures 4.3 and 4.4). Why did the children in school under these different managements show such significant differences in their social values and attitudes? The results suggested two possible informal sources of such differential social learning:

Figure 4.3
Children's Authoritarianism and Modernity by School Management

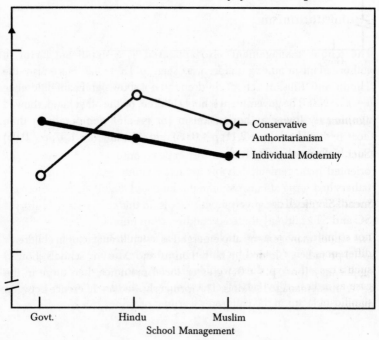

Figure 4.4
Children's Self-image and Social Attitudes by School Management

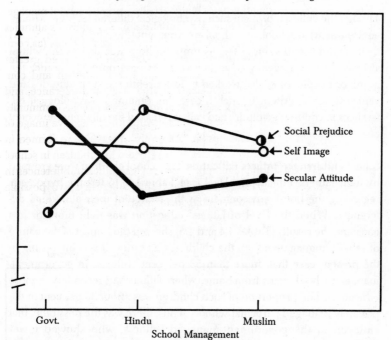

Impact of Home Environment

Such parochially-managed (in this case communally and parochially-oriented management) schools attracted children from homes where fathers had some affinity with the thinking and attitudes of the 'management'. Similarly, the government schools (in this case catering mostly to SC and ST children) attracted children from homes where fathers were not so much parochially inclined. Thus, such 'home'-learnt attitudinal differences were carried by children to their respective schools. Under such a case, the hypothesis would be that the home environment (in this case as indicated by fathers' education) was the major (if not the only) significant factor in the children's learning of values and attitudes.

Impact of School Environment

Though the children brought such psychological differences (due to home environment) to school, the school environment (the ethos) also impacted their attitudes and values. The assumption here was that as the school also works as an agency of socialisation, its environment, besides the home or in spite of it, also worked to foster/reinforce such attitudes and values in the children. In such a case, the obtained psychological differences in children's attitudes and values reflected the difference in school environments.

School Children by Fathers' Education The school children were grouped by their fathers' educational level (see Table 4.3) to test the hypothesis regarding the home environment as the source of their attitudinal differences. When the level of fathers' education was held more or less constant, the results (Tables 4.4 and 4.5) showed the impact of the nature of school 'management' on the children's attitudes. It was interesting in the present case that, more than 53 per cent children in government-managed schools came from homes where fathers had secondary or more education. The proportion of such children was about 36 per cent in the privately-managed parochial schools. Thus, there was the possibility that children in the government-managed schools, who showed lower authoritarianism (or higher democratism) and lower out-group prejudice, did so because a larger number of them came from homes where fathers had secondary or more education as compared to the other schools where fathers were less educated. Data in Tables 4.4 and 4.5, however, definitely nullifies such an explanation.

Table 4.3
Distribution of Children for School 'Management' by Fathers' Educational Level

School Management	Fathers' Educational Level				
	Low		High		
	Illiterate	Some Educated	Secondary	Higher	N
(Private) 'Hindu' managed	11	21	9	7	48
(Private) 'Muslim' managed	10	19	10	9	48
Government managed	8	36	47	3	94

Table 4.4
Authoritarianism, Secularism and Social Prejudice in Children of 'High' Educated Fathers by School

School Management	Children		Mean Scores on	
	N	CAA	SA	Out-group Prejudice
Government	50	52.7	27.0*	50.9
Private parochial	35	55.5**	24.5	55.3**

Notes: *Significant at 0.05 level.
**Significant at 0.01 level.

Table 4.5
Authoritarianism, Secularism and Social Prejudice in Children of Less Educated Fathers by School

School Management	N	Mean Scores on		
		CAA	SA	Out-group Prejudice
Government	44	53.2	26.4**	51.7
Private	61	58.2**	23.8	57.0**

Notes: *Difference significant at 0.01 level.

The fathers' education, as reported earlier, appeared as a significant factor in the formation of children's values and attitudes. However, with this factor controlled, the government-managed school children showed significantly different social attitudes from those in the parochially-managed private schools. All children, whether of more educated fathers (see Table 4.4) or of less educated fathers (see Table 4.5) in government-managed schools showed significantly lower authoritarianism, higher secularism and lower social (out-group) prejudice than those in the parochially-managed private schools.

The findings suggested that either the government-managed schools did something, may be more informally than formally, to enhance secularism and democratism, or the parochially-managed private schools did something to obtain the opposite in the children. Another possibility was that the teachers in this set of schools behaved differently in their respective classrooms while teaching the same formal curriculum.[12] The findings showed the impact and importance of the overall environment and ambience obtaining in the given set of schools for the children's attitudes and values. This hypothesis was stoutly supported by the findings seen in Tables 4.6 and 4.7. When the factor of school 'management' was controlled, i.e., within the respective set of schools, either within government-managed (Table 4.6) or within parochially-managed private schools

(Table 4.7), there was no difference in the attitudes of children of more educated fathers and those of less educated fathers.

Table 4.6

Authoritarianism, Secularism and Social Prejudice in Children in Government-managed Schools by Fathers' Education

Fathers' Education	N	Mean Scores on		
		CAA	SA	Out-group Prejudice
High	50	52.7	27.0	50.9
Low	44	53.2	26.4	51.7

Notes: No mean difference is significant.

Table 4.7

Authoritarianism, Secularism and Social Prejudice in Children in Parochially Managed Private Schools by Fathers' Education

Fathers' Education	N	Mean Scores on		
		CAA	SA	Out-group Prejudice
High	35	56.5	24.5	55.3
Low	61	58.2	23.8	57.0

Notes: No mean difference is significant.

There was, thus, strong evidence for the importance of school environment in the social learning of children. The influence of home environment seemed to wither away under the impact and influence of school ambience. The findings confirmed the importance of both home and school as significant sources of children's learning of social attitudes and values like authoritarianism, secularism and out-group prejudice. However, of these two, ambience and the general environment obtaining in school appeared to be more potent factors. The parochially-managed private schools were found to enhance authoritarianism, reduce secularism and promote greater social prejudice in their children. The secularising and democratising influence of educated fathers' homes also withered away under the powerful impact of the stimuli provided by the parochialising schools. It was also equally, if not more, important that the parochialising influence of home (of low educated fathers) seemed to give way to the secularising influence of the ambience obtaining in government-managed schools. While the parochially oriented 'Hindu' and 'Muslim' managed schools were found to wipe out the secular home influence, the government-managed schools eliminated the parochial home influence and helped the children imbibe liberal democratic attitudes. The finding was extremely important in view of the widespread illiteracy and lack of schooling among parents in the country. Secularly and democratically managed schools could become a potent source of democratisation and secularisation. The reverse was equally true. The parochially-managed schools could greatly derail this process and divert society into the opposite direction.[13] We discuss this matter further in Chapter 7.

Interaction of Home and School: Testing of Hypotheses

Home and School Environment

The home and the school provide most of the stimuli for children's growth. The school-going child breathes, plays and learns under such conditions. As discussed earlier, two types of home environment were assumed for the present study—parochial and secular (as indicated in this case by the fathers' educational level). Similarly, the school environment was also categorised as either parochial or secular (in this case as indicated by the nature of the school 'management'). These categories were discrete rather than continuous. The interaction of these categories created four possible conditions of a child's life. These could be labelled as follows:

(1) **Parochial-Parochial Environment (PPE)**–Here both the conditions (i.e., the environments at school and home) were parochial;

(2) **Parochial-Secular Environment (PSE)**–Here, the school conditions were parochial and the home conditions secular;

(3) **Secular-Parochial Environment (SPE)**–Here, the school conditions were secular and the home conditions parochial; and

(4) **Secular-Secular Environment (SSE)**–Here, the home as well as the school conditions were secular.

Although the environmental categories were discrete, the four types of child's environment tended to fall on a continuum on a four-point scale from PPE to SSE.

Testing of Hypotheses

Communalisation–Secularisation of Children's Attitudes

It was hypothesised that children living and studying under conditions of PPE (i.e., under a parochial environment both at home and at school) were likely to show the greatest sense of authoritarianism, 'communalism' and social distance (as compared to other children). And, the children under SSE conditions (i.e., a secular environment both at home and at school) would show the least of such communally-oriented authoritarian attitudes.

These hypotheses were dramatically confirmed (see Figures 4.5 and 4.6). The PPE type conditions of life were found to be contributing significantly to the communalisation of children's attitudes and values. As the children's environment became more secular, the attitudes of liberal-democratism and social harmony also got strengthened. The findings summarised as follows thus carried, as mentioned before, far-reaching implications for social and political development in the country:

Figure 4.5
Children's Authoritarianism and Secular Attitudes by Environment

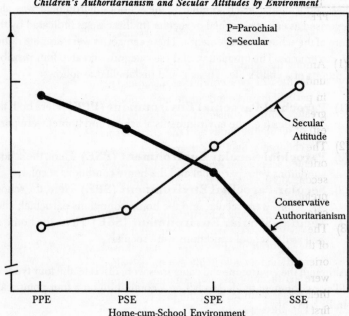

P=Parochial
S=Secular

Secular
Attitude

Conservative
Authoritarianism

PPE   PSE   SPE   SSE
Home-cum-School Environment

Figure 4.6
Children's Modernity and Social Prejudice by Environment

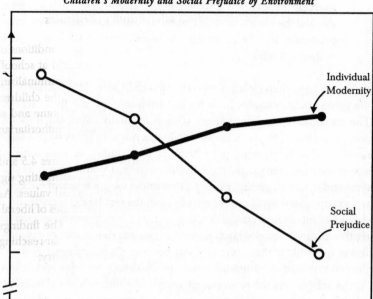

(1) Among the school children under study, those being brought up under the PPE type conditions, i.e., those living as well as studying in parochially-oriented home and school conditions, showed the greatest sense of conservative authoritarianism, lowest level (weakest) of secular attitudes and the greatest social prejudice.

(2) The children in the PSE category, i.e., those studying in parochially-oriented school and living in secularly-oriented home were placed second on the high to low scale of authoritarianism and on social prejudice. They were only somewhat lower than those in the first category, i.e., living and studying under PPE conditions.

(3) The reverse was the case (as compared to PSE category) in respect of the children of SPE category (i.e., those studying in secularly-oriented school while living in a parochially-oriented home). They were significantly less authoritarian, communal and prejudiced in their social attitudes than the first two categories, particularly the first category of children.

(4) The children under the SSE category (i.e., those living as well as studying in secularly-oriented home and school environments) showed the lowest sense of communal-authoritarianism and social prejudice, and the greatest sense of secularism and democratism in their attitudes.

The findings, thus, clearly showed that the child seemed to learn/acquire the given social attitudes from his/her environment, mostly at school. The communally-oriented private schools (in many cases, aided by the state) were found to play a major role in this respect. There were a large number of privately-managed schools in the country, at least some of which were being managed by religiously oriented 'communal' organisations under various garbs.[14] In the present study, the government-managed schools appeared significantly better as far as the secular-democratic social development of children was concerned. There was, however, no guarantee that all government schools showed the secular-democratic orientation. It was quite likely that some of them became parochially-oriented and thus contributed to communalisation of children's attitudes and values. As the school was the most potent source of children's social learning, schooling and the school management, as present research showed, played a crucial role in democratisation (or communalisation) of children's and, therefore, citizens' social attitudes and values with far-reaching implications for the society and polity of the country.

Modernity and Social Prejudice

As reported earlier, psychological modernity and social prejudice did not show any correlation. Thus, a socially-prejudiced person was not necessarily more traditional or less 'modern' in values. A psychologically 'modern' person could as well be highly socially prejudiced. Such a phenomenon was confirmed by the findings regarding children's attitudes and their social environment. Both the parochially-oriented as well as the secularly-oriented school-cum-home environment seemed to equally foster such psychological modernity in children (see Figure 4.6). The responses to modernity items were more cognitive in nature than the items in other instruments (see Annexure I). The out-group attitudinal items particularly evoked more affective responses. Similarly, the items of communal authoritarianism also seemed to evoke some kind of emotional response. The informal school environment, therefore, seemed to make a significant difference, particularly in the affective social learning of authoritarianism, communalism and social prejudice.[15]

The relationship (or the lack of it) between individual psychological modernity (as measured by the OM scale, as was the case in the present study) has been found to be highly related to 'factory' and school experience, so much so that each year of schooling added to the modernity score and that, 'men learnt to be more modern year by year after they entered factory' (Inkeles and Smith, 1974: 167). The individual modernity of this type was, therefore, likely to increase with increasing education and industrialisation. Will such 'modernity' promote social changes in developing countries like India? The development of a secular democratic society requires an enriching social environment and ideology. The growth of business and industries and the spread of formal school education could lead to modernity but would not automatically lead to the learning and spread of a secular democratic ideology.[16] On the contrary, the present research showed a real possibility of the growth of communal, non-egalitarian and authoritarian ideology of social prejudice in children despite their becoming psychologically modern. School and other secondary sources could be used to inculcate communal and authoritarian ideology. This could thus pose a serious threat to the development of a secular and democratic society and polity in the country.

Social Prejudice and Social Groups

Social environment, as reported earlier, showed significant relationship with children's prejudice. Did the social group (community) of the child make any difference in his/her social prejudice or in the sense of social distance with the 'other'? What was the extent of such mutually perceived social distances among the children from the various social groups? The semantic differential profiles of self-group and other groups were used to answer questions such as these. Distance (D) is the measure of relationship between the given groups as suggested by Osgood et al. (1957). Larger the D between any two social groups, greater is the psychological discrimination between them in the semantic space.

Four social groups of children were involved in the present study—the caste Hindu, the Muslim, the SC (Harijan/Dalits) and the ST (tribals). How did they perceive each other and themselves? What qualities did they attribute to WE, as a group and to THEY, as others? The obtained median scores on the semantic scales for the four groups were presented geometrically in the form of profiles to answer these questions.

Figure 4.7 presents the median scores of the caste Hindu children on the semantic differential scales. The first profile, from left to right, shows their self-image as a group, the middle two profiles represent their images of the SCs (Harijans) and the STs (tribals), and the last one shows their image of the Muslims. The images are arranged from very positive to very negative on a seven-point scale. The self-image of the caste Hindu children, as seen in the figure, was uniformly highly positive and their images of the tribals and the Harijans, almost neutral. Dramatically opposite were, however, their images of the Muslims. These were uniformly negative on all the adjectives.

Figure 4.7
Semantic Profiles of the Caste Hindu Children for Self and Others

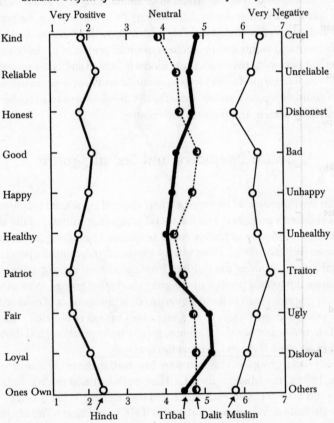

Operationally, the wider the gap between the self-image and the image of others, the greater is the psychological distance between the two. The amount of such distance shows the given in-group's perceived discrimination of the out-groups. Figures 4.7 to 4.10 show the perceived inter-group distances.

Figure 4.8
Semantic Profiles of the Muslim Children for Self and Others

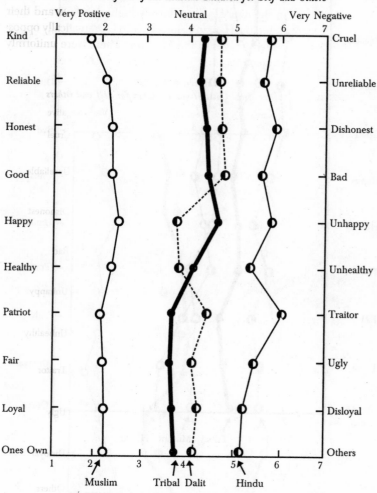

Figure 4.9
Semantic Profiles of the SC (Dalit) Muslim Children for Self and Others

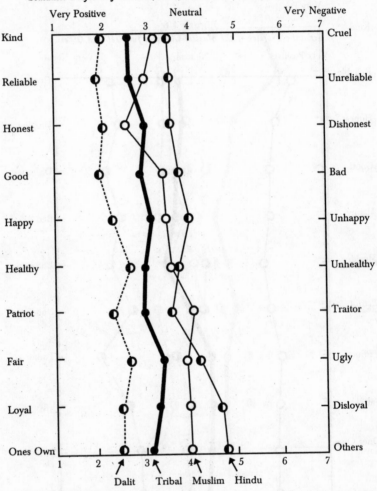

Figure 4.10
Semantic Profiles of the Tribal Children for Self and Others

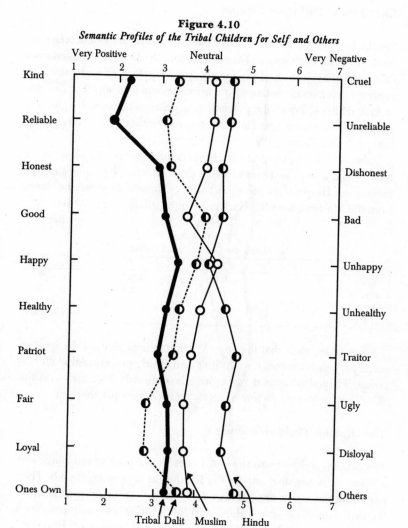

The Perceived Social Distance

The 'Hindu' Children's Images

On the basis of the semantic differential data, separate D-matrices were worked out for each group. For each matrix, the D was calculated from the in-group evaluation of the out-groups. Therefore, in each table, the reported D is a linear distance from the respective in-group. The first row in each matrix indicates the psychological distance between the given in-group and others, whereas the remaining rows indicate the perceived distance of 'others' among the rest of the groups.

Table 4.8 shows that the caste Hindu children perceived all the three other social groups at a considerable distance from their in-group, i.e., themselves. However, as was expected, they showed the greatest distance from the Muslims, then the Harijans and the tribals, in that order.

Table 4.8
D-Matrix for Caste Hindu Children

Social Groups	1	2	3	4
1. Hindu	–	6.12	4.97	4.37
2. Muslim			3.231	3.49
3. SCs			–	0.82
4. Tribal				–

It was, thus, clear that the caste Hindu children showed the greatest social prejudice towards the Muslims and clearly perceived it as an out-group. They also showed some prejudice towards the tribals and the SCs. They perceived their own social group in very positive light.

The 'Muslim' Children's Images

The Muslim children also showed a consistently positive self-image and a consistently negative one for the Hindus, as seen in Figure 4.8. They perceived the tribals and the SCs at, more or less, equidistance. Thus, the two groups, i.e., the 'Hindu' and the 'Muslim' mutually perceived each other as 'traitor', 'unreliable', 'dishonest' and 'unhealthy'. However, the median values suggested (see Figures 4.7 and 4.8) that the caste Hindu children harboured greater hostility (prejudice) towards the 'Muslims' than was the case vice versa.

Table 4.9 also reveals more or less the same pattern as in Table 4.8. However, the magnitude of the distance perceived by Muslims for Hindus was less as compared to the one perceived by the caste Hindu children for the Muslims. The Muslim children showed the greatest distance from the caste Hindus, followed by the tribals and the SCs (Harijans). However, the social distance perceived by the caste Hindu children towards Harijans and the tribals was much more than that perceived by the Muslim children for such groups.

Table 4.9
D-Matrix for the Muslim Children

Groups	1	2	3	4
1. Hindu	–	5.38	3.89	4.07
2. Muslim		–	1.86	2.13
3. SCs			–	0.63
4. Tribal				–

The 'Harijan' Children's Images

Figure 4.9 shows the attitudes of the SC ('Harijan'/Dalit) children towards their own and the three other social groups. Though they perceived themselves most favourably, interestingly, at the same time, they evaluated other groups also in positive light.

As seen in Table 4.10, the quantum of social distance shown by the Dalit children for other social groups was much less than that shown by the Hindu and the Muslim children. Interestingly, the Dalits showed the greatest distance from Hindus and then, from Muslims. They (Dalits) did not perceive Hindus as 'their own' and were doubtful whether they were 'loyal'. On the other hand, they felt a greater sense of identification with tribals and Muslims than with Hindus. The Dalits' image of tribals was definitely positive. They perceived them as 'good', 'reliable', 'kind', and 'patriotic'. The Dalits' image of Hindus and vice versa, as seen in Figures 4.7 and 4.9 was almost identical. Attitudinally, the Dalits attributed more positive qualities to themselves than to Hindus and vice versa. It was interesting that the 12–year old Dalit children did not perceive 'caste Hindus', the dominant social group, as their reference group, i.e., the object of their imitation and as the model for their behaviour. Such emerging Dalit attitudes and their image of the caste Hindus raised doubt about the validity of the concept of Sanskritisation.[17]

Table 4.10
D-Matrix for the Harijan Children

Groups	1	2	3	4
1. Hindu	–	2.32	1.78	1.12
2. Muslim		–	0.93	1.82
3. SCs			–	0.94
4. Tribal				–

The Tribal Children's Images

The concept of Sanskritisation further came into question by the findings regarding the tribal children's image of Hindus, as seen in Figure 4.10. It was more or less uniformly on the neutral to the negative side. The tribal image of the Muslims was more positive than that of the Hindus. The latter stood farthest on the tribal children's attitudinal scale. On the other hand, their self-image and those for the Harijans (Dalits) embraced each other. Interestingly, the children of the two oppressed social groups felt in tune with each other and thought positively of themselves. Their perceived closeness to the Muslims, as seen in Table 4.11, also probably indicated their psychological proximity to other oppressed people. The main oppressors of Harijans and the tribals have traditionally come from among the upper caste Hindus—the Thakurs, Brahmins and the Banias (money-lenders). The oppressed class children felt proud of themselves, while the 'oppressor' high caste group worked as negative reference groups for them. Such attitudes found among them in the early 1970s were opposite of those found in 1950 and even in the 1960s, when studies showed the Harijan and tribal children to have positive images of the Hindus.[18] This possible shift in the attitudes of Dalits and tribals in the span of just one to two decades was of great social and political significance. Such attitudes among children from traditionally-marginalised social groups were probably reflected in their changing political behaviour in the 1990s (see Chapter 1).

Table 4.11
D-Matrix for the Tribal Children

Groups	1	2	3	4
Hindu	–	2.51	1.42	0.67
Muslim		–	1.21	1.83
SCs			–	1.02
Tribal				–

The findings yielded the following important conclusions: (*a*) The caste Hindu children exhibited the greatest social prejudice of all. They showed remarkable psychological distance from the Muslims and considerable distance from the tribals and the SCs. (*b*) The Muslim children also showed equally strong prejudice against the Hindus and the other two groups. (*c*) The SC children felt closest to the tribals and farthest from the caste Hindus. However, their prejudice towards the Hindus was much less than that of the Hindus for them. (*d*) The tribals showed closest affinity with the SCs and farthest distance from the caste Hindus. (*e*) All children, including the Harijans and the tribals, uniformly perceived their own group in a positive light. (*f*) The results indicated a shift in the attitudes of oppressed class children towards the higher caste groups and towards themselves. They now felt proud of themselves and negative of the caste Hindus from whom came their main social oppressors. Such attitudes among the children in the early 1970s carried important implications for development, democratisation and nation-building in the years to come (see Chapter 1).

Social Class and Children's Social Learning

The STs and the SCs have historically been underprivileged social classes.[19] For centuries, they have been denied access to education, occupational mobility, equality of opportunity, and to lead a decent human life.[20] These in effect have meant denial of their basic rights. Despite some government measures to help them,[21] the plight of such exploited people has not improved much.[22] Contextually, therefore, it was remarkable that the SC and ST children showed less manifest authoritarianism than the caste Hindu and the Muslim children. Though they showed a sense of distance from caste Hindus and Muslims, more so with the former, and also harboured a negative image of them, on the whole, however, they manifested much less out-group hostility than other more privileged social groups. They also showed less implicit authoritarianism than other children. Combining the two (i.e., the implicit and manifest authoritarianism), the deprived social class children showed a more progressive (as against conservative) and democratic (as against authoritarian) political orientation than the caste Hindu and Muslim children.

It is important to note here that the SCs and STs belonged to the lowest rung of the Indian society and that about 90 per cent of the government school children included in the present study, belonged to this extremely deprived social class.[23] Interestingly, more than half the fathers of such children were educated upto secondary or higher level. Most of these children were, therefore, likely to be socialised by secular-secular environment (SSE). Their fathers' upward social mobility and rising aspirations, and their schools' liberal social environment could have contributed to their socially liberal and democratic political orientation. Western studies, mostly in USA, have tended to show a higher sense of authoritarianism in working class parents and their children than those belonging to the middle class. The former have been found to be liberal on economic issues and authoritarian on non-economic issues.[24] It was, therefore, remarkable that contrary to such Western findings, children originating in homes which have traditionally belonged to the 'labouring class' showed greater tolerance of others and greater sense of equality in social terms than the traditionally 'lower-middle class' children. They were more liberal and progressive, not only in economic terms (economic equality, desirability of nationalisation' etc.) but also in social terms, than the latter. They (the lower class children) were, in fact, attitudinally closer to the more educated 'middle class' children in respect of political and civic issues. They were lower on implicit and manifest authoritarianism than those originating in the less educated lower middle class.

Social Mobility among SCs and Tribals

The fathers' occupational position could have some influence on their children's attitudes. More than 80 per cent fathers of children in the government-managed schools, as seen in Table 4.12, were employed in jobs such as clerks, teachers, peons and watchmen. Some of them were also lawyers and petty government officials. Only a small number of fathers, about 14 per cent, were self-employed and worked as petty shop-keepers or in some petty service job. Designating teachers, clerks, lawyers, etc., as 'middle class', and peons, watchmen, workers as lower class, nearly half the children in the government schools came from middle class and another half from lower class homes. Applying the same occupational criteria, majority of the children in the parochially-managed private schools came from lower middle class homes. It appeared, therefore, that the government-managed schools (in the present study in the early 1970s) attracted children more from the 'middle class' and/or lower class

SC and ST homes. On the other hand, the parochially-managed private schools attracted more children from lower middle class Hindu or Muslim homes. Government schools also attracted children from the working class much more than private schools. Typically, the government schools catered (in the present study, i.e., in the early 1970s) more to the SC and ST children and those from middle class and lower (working) class homes, while the privately-managed parochial schools, more to the lower middle class children. Assuming that, for most SCs and STs, jobs such as clerks, peons, etc., were probably the first generation jobs, these marked a big change in their lives.[25] For them—the oppressed and marginalised, some as untouchables, for ages—such jobs symbolised mobility and high social prestige despite the fact that these were very low in the occupational prestige hierarchy.[26]

The newly acquired educational status and a salaried job, preferably in government, therefore, marked a quantum jump for the SC and ST people, contributing greatly to their values and aspirations.[27] Such social and occupational changes contributed to creating a conducive home environment for the learning of liberal, secular and democratic attitudes and values by their children. Such attitudes and values were further reinforced by the secularly-oriented government managed schools.

The Lower Middle (Business) Class

Most fathers in the lower middle class (see Table 4.12) were engaged in some small business and/or in some petty self-employed work. Such occupations could have been higher (than e.g., peons) in the occupational hierarchy. They might have also been earning more. Probably, they may have been engaged in such trade/work for generations. The nature of their work and also lack of mobility, however, tended to create a conservative authoritarian political orientation in them. Interestingly, near about the same time as of the present study, this class of voters were found, during an election campaign, to recall significantly greater conservative themes. They also showed greater response to such themes.[28] The nature of the fathers' occupation and comparatively their lower level of education on the one hand, and the parochial school environment on the other, probably reinforced each other in promoting social learning of conservative authoritarianism, communalism and social prejudice in the children.

Table 4.12

Distribution of Children for School by Fathers' Occupational (Social) Class

Occupation	Designated Social Class	Children in Schools			
		Government Managed (Mostly SCs & STs)	'Hindu' Managed (Mostly Caste Hindus)	'Muslim' Managed (Mostly Muslims)	Total
Clerks, teachers, lawyers, etc.	Middle	40	14	10	64
Small business, shop-keepers, self-employed	Lower Middle	12	25	27	64
Workers including peons, watchmen, etc.	Lower	42	9	11	62
Number of Cases		**94**	**48**	**48**	**190**

The White Collar Middle Class

Nearly one-third of the total sample of children came from white collar middle class homes of clerks, teachers, lawyers, etc. Out of these, nearly two-thirds, as seen in Table 4.12, were in the government-managed schools. These were the better educated fathers. As reported earlier (See Tables 4.6 and 4.7), the children of such 'middle class' homes showed no significant difference either on implicit or on manifest authoritarianism irrespective of their school group. The findings suggested that such children, mostly studying in government schools, were qualitatively different from the lower middle class homes, studying mostly in private schools. The former group of children showed significantly lower authoritarianism than the latter. In case of the former, a white collar middle class job could mean a release of hope and aspiration for a better life, while in case of the latter, petty shopkeeping or trade did not make any such difference. On the contrary, continuation in such usual jobs could mean conservation of status quo. Such differences in the conditions of life could have, on the one hand, contributed to promoting liberalism, secularism and social understanding in the SC and ST children and, on the other, reinforced a sense of conservative authoritarianism in other children.

Children's Social Learning

Children's social and political learning takes place not much through formal curriculum and classroom teaching, though it is also an important factor. Most schools follow the same curriculum, use the same books and follow the same system of examination and certification. Yet, some of them secularise and some others communalise children's attitudes. The difference, as the present study showed, stems from the environment and the 'ideological' ethos of the school. The nature of school 'management' plays a crucial role in this respect. From time to time, attempts have been made to curb such communal and parochial tendencies, albeit only at the textbook level (NCERT, 1961; and Nomani, 1968). The problem is, however, much deeper, which warrants attention to a whole range of activities. As Bronfenbrenner (1962) and Dunn and Dunn (1962) have shown, rapid development and the desired political change depended heavily upon conscious manipulation of both the formal as well as the informal school environment. This became all the more important as more and more children from lower class homes entered our schools. For many of them, it could be the first generation education and their home environment might not be conducive to developing liberal-democratic and secular values and attitudes. In their case, the school, therefore, assumed a double role. On the other hand, if such children entered a 'parochially'-managed school, they were likely to be socialised at variance to the national goals of secular democracy. The school, there-fore, is the key both ways. It could become a conscious instrument of national integration and democratic-secular development. Or it could become a tool for inculcating/reinforcing authoritarian and communal attitudes and behaviour in children, thus greatly contributing to the com-munal divide in the country.

Implications for Democratisation and Development

The present study generally confirmed the importance of home and the school in socialisation of children. The role of education in national inte-gration and development has been discussed repeatedly since independ-ence (Gautam, 1970; Naik, 1965; NCERT, 1961; Ramnathan, 1965). The Education Commission (1964–66) even titled its report as 'Education and National Development' (Government of India, 1966). The role of the school in children's social learning was never in doubt. The real question is socialisation towards what. The findings here raised some disturbing questions in this regard. Do our schools, at least some of the parochially-managed schools, communalise children's attitudes? Do they promote democratisation or do they inculcate and/or reinforce psychological distance and hostility among the children of various social groups? The results showed that there were quite a few schools (in the early 1970s) which tended to communalise and de-democratise children's attitudes and behaviour (albeit with government aid). Such findings following serious communal violence during that period, in the late 1960s and early 1970s, suggested far-reaching implications for social harmony in the country, as some subsequent events, as discussed in Chapter 1, showed. The children from Dalit homes—the SCs and the tribals—harboured not only lower social distance from other social groups on the whole, but also showed greater psychological identity among themselves. Thus, the SC children felt mentally closer to the tribals and also the Muslim children, suggesting greater affinity with each other than with the caste Hindu children. Such children, i.e., those from lower social class homes, also showed greater attachment to democratic and secular values and attitudes. Such attitudes during the late 1960s and early 1970s among the Dalit children were symptomatic of a rising sense of efficacy and democratic aspirations in them. Such trends, in a way, could predict the emerging democratic changes in the country, as discussed in Chapter 1. The 12–13-year old children—the respondents in the present study in 1972–73—grew into full adulthood in the 1990s, the period during which Dalits have tended to reveal dramatic changes in their political behaviour. It is no wonder that the political paradigm seems to be changing with the dispossessed and deprived social groups showing greater sense of efficacy, assertion and political interest than the elite groups (see Chapter 1).

The study of children's behaviour and the socialisation processes, thus, tended to show two contradictory, maybe dialectical, social tendencies. On the one hand, children primarily from the upper caste groups tended to show communally-oriented authoritarian attitudes, and on the other, those from the lower social groups tended to show secular and democratically-oriented attitudes. These trends probably symbolised the parallel processes of communalisation and democratisation underway in the country at the same time (see Chapter 1). One thing was, however, clear. A significant change in the self-concepts of children from the traditionally oppressed groups was underway. Such changes were likely to boost not only their aspirations but also generate demand and pressure from below for better governance and performance, as found during the

1990s (see Chapter 1). Such changes, therefore, indicated the need for a new development paradigm and, more importantly, new leadership and problem-solving behaviour. We discuss some of these developmental issues in the subsequent chapters.

Notes

1. A brief version of this study was published as a paper, see Rao and Mehta 1979.
2. For example, see Anant 1972; Bhusan 1967; Bronfenbrénner 1958; Himmelweit; Inkeles 1966; Kohn 1969; Lipset 1960; Mehta 1969; and Williams 1960. These studies found significant relationship between social class and certain important socio-political values and attitudes.
3. Kuppuswamy 1962 has prepared a socio-economic scale based on person's education, occupation and income, standardised in the early 1950s on university students. This scale has been used in several studies since then. Its principal difficulty has been the possibility of correct information on income, in the absence of which the scale gives misleading picture. Also, education and occupation show very high positive correlation, and both with the composite SES. Thus, Mehta 1969 found $r = 0.754$ between educational level and occupational position, and the two showed r's of 0.820 and 0.815 (in all cases, $N = 844$) with the composite SES (Mehta 1969: 57). Many years ago, Cattle 1942 also reported that social prestige had $r = 0.93$ with income and $r = 0.87$ with years of education.
4. See Hyman 1959; Kohn 1969; and Lipset 1960 for similar results. The lower educated fathers and the lower class uniformly tended to show greater conservative authoritarianism.
5. For detailed discussion of education and modernity, see Inkeles and Smith 1974; Portes 1973; Weiner 1966. Inkeles and Smith (pp. 237–47) found highly significant correlations with children's OM scores and their fathers' education in several countries with median correlation of 0.33. This could be an artifact of correlation between fathers' and sons' education. Through matching, etc., correlations disappeared in two countries. In India, Argentina and Chile, it continued to show significant correlation.
6. Sumner 1906 has emphasised the in-group or self image in describing ethnocentric tendencies. See also Allport (1958: 42), who has speculated about the potency of widening in-group circles. For an empirical demonstration of the generality of out-group rejection and in-group liking, see Adorno 1950.
7. For relationship between education and prejudice, see Adorno 1950; Anant 1972; and Shankar 1966.
8. See Kohn 1969: 19–37, for discussion regarding self-direction, conformism and social class.
9. Kohn 1969; has discussed at length the influence of social structure on behaviour, and found education as well as occupation, significantly related to values. Education was more potent of the two, showing a strong relationship with parental values, particularly with authoritarian conservatism (pp. 130–32).

10. School has the potentiality to inculcating inter-group hostility through conscious, planned instruction, as well as through informal casual experiences provided by the school milieu. For discussion, see Parsons 1959; see discussion of manifest and latent functions of school in Merton (1959: 50–84). In addition to the curriculum itself, the school climate, peer groups and teachers contribute to the formation of inter-group attitudes at school. In this regard, see an early report by Hess and Easten 1962; Holes 1951; and National Education Association of USA 1940.

11. For discussion of such gains on the OM scale, see Inkeles and Smith (1974: 135–43). The progress of modernisation is directly related to the pace of educational advancement and the one sure way to modernise quickly is to modernise the curriculum. The Kothari Commission (1964–66) strongly emphasises this need (see particularly, para 1.69 and p. 17). It has also emphasised the need for democratisation and secularisation of education (Government of India, 1966). Also see Anderson 1966 and Shills 1966. Dube 1974 has analysed this process in the Indian context.

12. For understanding classroom behaviour, see Mehta 1967–68 and for review of research on classroom behaviour, see Rao and Mehta 1973.

13. See Warkov and Greeley 1966 for a detailed discussion of parochial school origins and educational achievement, and Sharma 1969 for organisational climates of private and government-managed schools. Almond and Verba (1963: 363–73) have given data to show that education upto secondary level and above, can replace family participation as a factor leading towards development of political competence.

14. During 1967–68, there were in all 517,508 schools in the country, of which 97,417 were private-aided and 10,246 private-unaided schools. The influence of the private management in school education increases with increasing level of schooling. It can be understood by the fact that (during 1967–68) there were 18,952 aided and 1,800 unaided private secondary schools out of the total 31,713 secondary schools in the country. See Government of India (1974: 70–74).

15. Langton 1969 has reported on a national survey of high school seniors in USA. The study centred on the relationship between the number of civics courses taken and the students' political knowledge and sophistication, interest in political discussions, media consumption, sense of efficacy and cynicism, as well as their level of civic tolerance. The results offered little support for the impact of the curriculum even as a minor source of political socialisation. Among the entire sample, they did not find a single case in which civics training was significantly associated with students' political orientation (pp. 85–119). He reported a typical pattern in the United States where certain constellations of family characteristics were important in moving children from low to a medium level of political interest. The family seemed to have reached the zenith of its influence at this point. Thereafter, other secondary agencies with certain identifiable characteristics were required to move children to a higher level of political interest (p. 173).

16. See Smith 1965 for an interesting discussion of this point. He argues that the ideology has to be inculcated. Citing the example of USSR, he says,

For whatever they may seem to say, clearly, they have in fact believed that in order to change society one must change men's minds. So also China. It is only idealist Indian and the un-Marxist West that in practice seem to imagine that the modernisation of economics can precede the modernisation of popular outlook (p. 30).

17. See Srinivas (1971: 1–45). He says, 'Sanskritisation is a process by which a "low" Hindu caste or tribal or other group changes its customs, rituals, ideology and way of life in the direction of a high and frequently "twice born castes"' (p. 6).

18. Several studies were contributed during the 1950s and 1960s on stereotypes, social tension and social prejudices. The results showed consistently that socially-oppressed classes, such as the SCs and STs were uniformly negatively perceived by themselves while they tended to positively evaluate Hindus, Muslims, Christian, etc. For contributions, see Pareek 1971.

19. For the status of such social classes, see Cattle 1942; Ghurye 1957; Neugarten 1946; and Warner 1949.

20. There is a large body of literature on the plight of such social classes in the country. Incidents of atrocities on them, in fact, have been multiplying alarmingly in different parts of the country. Rape, loot, and even murder have been common features. See Lynch 1969; Murthy et al. 1969, for such information and discussion.

21. For a historical review of these measures, see Natraj 1959 and for some recent information, see Issack 1964.

22. For trends in social mobility among such deprived communities, see Chauhan 1955. For politics behind such trends, see Lynch 1969 and Vidyarthi 1971.

23. For a critical evaluation of the life of such deprived classes, see Mahar 1972 and Naik 1972.

24. See Hyman 1959. Lipset 1960 has suggested that in working class authoritarianism

the poorer everywhere are more liberal and leftist on economic issues, they favour more welfare state measures, higher wages, graduated income taxes, support trade unions and other measures opposed by those of higher class positions. On the other hand, when liberalism is defined on non-economic terms, the correlation is reversed (p. 485).

25. While analysing TAT stories written by class 9 boys in 1964 for need for achievement, I found several stories written by lower class boys, articulating the post of peon or some other similarly low post in the government as their career goal. This indicated the nature of their ambition as well as the attraction of such jobs for them (Mehta 1969). Also see Irring Krauss 1964 for educational aspirations among the lower social classes.

26. See Hollingshead and Fredrick 1958 for treatment of social class on the basis of education and occupational prestige. The latter may vary from culture to culture but the social stratification tends to follow social prestige hierarchy.

27. For results regarding social mobility, see Hyman 1959: 85. The data suggested that upward mobility produces an attenuation of parental influence interpretable in terms of new group membership norms.

28. See Mehta 1975b for data regarding electoral themes, policy slogans and the content of evoked response. The lower and upper class voters tended to recall radical themes, and shopkeepers (in the middle class, lower middle class, depending on how it is broken) showed greater recall of conservative themes.

Leadership, Problem-solving and Development Functioning: Instrumentation

As discussed in Chapter 1, there was a need to undertake research in order to help evaluate, monitor and improve various aspects of development practice on the ground. Though the traditional social organisation based on caste hierarchy is still entrenched, rather strongly, marginalised people have been increasingly asserting for their rights and for a due place in society. This is shown dramatically in the emerging competitive electoral politics where the traditional paradigm of authority is being challenged by the hitherto dominated people (see Chapter 1). However, there is widespread illiteracy, poverty and social backwardness in the country. There is an increasing concern among people for better performance and governance. They expect the state to play an entrepreneurial and empowering role in development. Even for neo-economic liberalisation, there is a need for the country to enhance its competitiveness and capability in order to compete in the changed circumstances. In such a context, the state and the various development functionaries, including non-government functionaries, need to use appropriate leadership styles so as to energise the social sector. They need to show a greater sense of social concern and readiness to help release initiative and develop capability in people. The traditional dominative leadership and exclusionary communication styles which really never worked (see Chapter 1), have become all the more counter-productive now. Development functioning and administrative and managerial styles have to be, therefore, in consonance with the changing times in order to achieve the desired results and the expected performance.

There is, thus, a need in this respect to understand leadership behaviour in the context of the national goals of strengthening democratic processes and practices and secular and scientific temper in the country. As discussed elsewhere (Mehta, forthcoming), there was (and is) always a gap between goals and theory of development and its practice on the ground. Despite repeated policy documents, such as for agricultural extension, rural development, labour welfare, literacy and primary education and health, the development practice on the ground has been rather frustrating. However, such dissonance between promises and practice, between word and the deed, is becoming more glaring and repulsive as people are becoming more and more concerned and, also, somewhat more demanding. Fulfilment of people's basic needs and the desired goals of development is, therefore, assuming much more urgency now. The desired development performance requires all-out efforts including research to understand people's needs, problems and aspirations on the one hand, and values, motivation and behaviours of the concerned functionaries, on the other. Also, specifically designed education and training based on such research could help reinforce and develop appropriate behaviours conducive to dealing with the various development tasks. The concerned officials and functionaries need to have a sense of belonging to their workplace and to the on-going development process. Such identification with development work and commitment to the goals would help them acquire and show greater sensitivity to the needs of the people, and greater readiness for promoting desired capability and competitiveness among the people. The present research was undertaken to understand development behaviours of the officials and the functionaries.

As a first step in the study, it was decided to develop instruments for assessing leadership values/styles, styles of dealing with people's development problems, readiness to assess administrative behaviour in current development functioning, and aspects of self-concept such as sense of initiative and autonomy, self-esteem and sense of reflective action. It was also decided to use already available instruments for assessing the sense of workplace satisfaction and some selected psychological needs of the functionaries. We briefly discuss now, the steps undertaken and some relevant data towards construction and validation of these instruments.

Construction of Instruments

Leadership Values/Styles Questionnaire (L-Scale)

The leadership questionnaire was constructed following the conceptualisation presented in Table 5.1. A sampling of situations was culled out from reports and notes of field surveys (Mehta, 1989a: 45–46, 92–95,

123–25; Mehta, 1995: 86–90, 127–31). An inventory of items/situations was then developed. After initial discussions with experts and a tryout, 10 such situations were selected, each followed by four responses of which the respondent was required to choose one. For instance, Situation 1 in the questionnaire reads:

> An organisation is engaged in providing vocational training. They offer courses in home-oriented skills like sewing, embroidery and knitting for women and courses in mechanical and technical trades such as repair of automobile and repair and manufacture of electronic goods, car driving, etc. for men. What do you think of such a training scheme for men and women?

Table 5.1

*Leadership for Empowerment: Values at Workplace
and in Development Conceptualisation*

Direct, Dominative Values/Styles	Indirect, Integrative Values/Styles
Prescriptive	Dialoguing.
Explaining; directing	Enabling people to transcend themselves via action and reflection.
Shaping climate where people are objects of control and domination	Shaping climate of critical discovery; awareness of humanising and dehumanising conditions.
Managing by narration; by banking; by depositing information	Bottom-up communication; coding and decoding; understanding; reasoning.
Work for and/or against people	Working with people.
Extracting; stimulating production	Setting challenging job; higher goals; total vision and parts as elements in the whole.

Source: Mehta (1998: 120–25).

The respondents were required to tick mark one of the following four responses:

(1) The organisation is right in offering such courses as these are usual choices of men and women.

(2) It is useful to assign them different courses suited to their nature as men and women. The organisation should continue to prescribe such courses for generating income.

(3) It is not a good scheme as there should be no difference between men and women in vocational training.

(4) It is a dysfunctional scheme as it is likely to reinforce and perpetuate gender discrimination in the society by preparing women for domesticated work and men for modern and market oriented work.

Table 5.2

Situations and Responses Indicating
Values and Beliefs in Leadership Behaviour Scale

Situation/Theme	Values/Attitudes/Beliefs Indicated by the Given Responses
Vocational training for men and women	Support gender discrimination; value gender equality; value women empowerment.
A villagers' meeting to consider use of seeds and methods of farming	Villagers are ignorant and lazy; allowing people to ask questions; value integrative communication for people's ideas and experiences.
A villagers' meeting to consider a health problem (malaria)	Villagers are ignorant, hence need instruction, lecturing on sanitation; showing sensitivity; value collective action.
Farmers faced with a crop disease	Justifying doling out inputs and information; patronising them for information; value discussion for developing capability.
A situation of chaos at the workplace	People do not want to work; they like to socialise; rewarding performance; value challenging and worthwhile work.
A villagers' meeting to discuss problems of water	People's grievances are never-ending; village meetings are a waste of time; enhancing awareness is good; empowering them for collective action.
Working as per guidelines at the workplace	Pleasing the boss and the head office; working by guidelines is good; implementation as per guidelines is important; value programme implementation with care and interest.
Discipline the workplace	A good officer gives directions; at a good workplace, people follow instructions; doubting whether this is a good workplace; value initiative and freedom for productive work.
Extra hard/and overtime work	People work only under supervision; people work hard when paid extra; extracting work is valued; value capability and initiative.
A school with absentee teachers	No harm if school remains closed; teachers need to be threatened; recommend dismissal and appoint new teachers; value public activism for better schooling.

The preferred response would indicate whether the respondent tends to favour traditional values informing gender discrimination and social inequality or the opposite, i.e., the values of gender equality in matters like education and vocational training.

Responses to other given situations indicated beliefs, values and attitudes such as: respect for people and their ideas and use of integrative communication with villagers, promotion of reflection and action-orientation in the community, support for worthwhile work and challenging environment at the workplace, workers' involvement and release of their initiative at the workplace, and people empowerment and public activism for development. Alternatively, the responses could also indicate the opposite of the values/attitudes/beliefs or a neutral stance in the given situation (see Table 5.2). Some of the items here were similar to an earlier instrument on faith in people and conservative dogmatism (Mehta, 1989b: 169–70). It also drew from earlier research on work-related values and social outlook (Mehta, 1994c: 153–68; Rao and Mehta, 1978).

The Four Possible Preferences

The responses provided for the sampled ten work and development situations could result in four possible value patterns and leadership styles, initially labelled as directive, prescriptive, educative and enabling or empowering. As each situation could be responded to in only one of the four given ways, the questionnaire, thus, yielded information on the relative strength of the preferred value pattern informing the respondent's likely leadership style. It was presumed that combination of directive and prescriptive responses would yield a score on dominative and a combination of the other two, on integrative leadership values/styles.

Development Problem-solving Scale (DPS Scale)

Development problem-solving scale consists of 10 statements, each containing some typical need of the people or some problem faced by them in general. These were culled out from a large number of problems and needs articulated by the people during fieldwork in reports of village-level group meetings, personal interviews and from discussions with villagers and other working people in various parts of the country (Mehta,

1995: 120–36, 186–95). Such problems are also well known and are often reported in the media and other forums. These problems reflect some well-known basic needs of the people, some of which also follow from the preamble, directive principles of the state policy, and the fundamental Rights enshrined in the constitution. Interestingly, as discussed in Chapter 1, people now tend to evaluate government in terms of such needs. These, therefore, should inform the goals/objectives of development programmes and the state policy in general.

Ten such pressing problems and needs, finally selected for the instrument, relate to: credit, health, employment, literacy, development functioning, forests and environment, water, alcoholism, slums and minimum wages. Each problem/statement is followed by four possible approaches of dealing with it. Two of the four responses show either a direct boss-like approach or an 'officious' bureaucratic approach to dealing with the problem—both typical of government functioning. The third approach to the problem could be to assist the community/people but without providing 'an actor' space to them. Another way could be that he/she opts to deal with the given problem so that the concerned people develop their own capability and acquire an actor role in the situation. For instance, for the given health problem, the respondent could deal with it by 'reporting it to the concerned department' or by 'approaching the health department for providing medicines' or 'lecture to the people about importance of sanitation and hygiene' or help people to identify causes of the problem, mobilise and 'demand' action from the concerned authorities so that the disease is prevented and eliminated. Although the given responses varied from problem to problem, the basic approaches to dealing with the people's development and other problems remained more or less the same. These were initially labelled as 'directive', 'prescriptive', 'educative' and 'empowering' styles. It was presumed that the first two approaches, i.e., 'directive' and 'prescriptive', would add up to a score on 'pawn'-inducing tendency and the other two, to an actor-promoting tendency in dealing with people's problems.

Sense of Personal Efficacy (SPE Scale)

Sense of personal efficacy is a self-concept scale which contains 15 items, five each for three dimensions, namely, sense of initiative and autonomy (vs. dependency), sense of self-esteem (vs. self-depreciation) and sense of reflective action (vs. repetitive behaviour).

Sense of autonomy-dependency includes items on initiative, hope of success, problem-solving, fear of failure and conformity. Sense of self-esteem–depreciation includes innovativeness, creativity, playing safe and security. Reflective action includes actor role, challenge and quality-seeking at work vs. tendency for routine mechanical labour. The instrument drew from earlier research with sense of political powerlessness and normlessness (Mehta, 1989a: 93–95 and 169–70) and sense of social efficacy (Mehta, 1975c, 1975d, 1977a, 1994c, 1996b: 159–60). The dimensions and the items were based on conceptualisation presented in Table 5.3.

Table 5.3

Aspects of Self-Concept Dimensions of Powerlessness and Efficacy Conceptualisation

Sense of Powerlessness Dimension	Sense of Personal Efficacy Dimension
Fear of Freedom; dependence; fear of failure	Autonomy; initiative; hope of success (expectation).
Conformity: problem-solving	Confronting reality: problem-solving.
Unable to take risk (security)	Moderate, calculated risk; innovativeness.
Pawns: submerged into reality	Actors: act, reflect and act; praxis; transcending self.
Self-depreciation: 'Being for Others'	Self-esteem: 'Being for Themselves'.
Physically stimulated to work, to labour	Challenged by job for quality performance; creativity.

Source: Mehta (1998: 105–10).

Release of initiative, autonomy, self-esteem and sense of reflective action also constitute important goals of human development, particularly in a country like India. Historically, people have been conditioned to the dependency syndrome which motivates them to fear freedom, seek conformity, avoid problem-solving, submerge into reality and behave like pawns, tending to self-depreciation and 'being' for others, and to being physically stimulated for labour. These have evolved, over the years, as important behavioral dimensions of the sense of powerlessness (Mehta, 1998: 85–92). Human development and education should therefore, as discussed in Chapter 1, aim at inculcating a sense of autonomy and initiative, hope of success, problem-solving approach, moderate risk-taking capability, actor-like behaviour, self-esteem and competence and motivation for seeking challenge and quality of work. Such behavioural dimensions of personal efficacy also constitute important elements in the 'pedagogy of the oppressed' (Freire, 1972).

As some action programmes and research studies show, political and social mobilisation and collective action help people overcome their traditional sense of dependency and powerlessness, and enhance their sense of personal efficacy and empowerment. Participatory development programmes and people's movements confirm such hypotheses, as briefly mentioned in Chapter 1 (Mehta, 1995: 163–80). However, development functionaries, whether government or non-government, involved in implementing empowerment and capability-related development programmes, themselves need to have sense of such personal efficacy. They need to have initiative, sense of self-worth and readiness for reflective action in order for them to help people develop such efficacy. The present questionnaire was, therefore, designed in two forms—Form A, to study and, if necessary, help develop such efficacy in development functionaries and Form B, for the community or the people with whom they work.

Development Functioning (Assessment) Questionnaire (DF Scale)

Reviews of development programmes and related research suggest the presence of certain dysfunctional administrative tendencies in development functioning on the ground. For instance, the officials have been found to show over-fondness for sheer number of activities, physical targets and expenditure and low concern for social objectives of various programmes and for quality in performance, and were reluctant to implement policy guidelines for promoting participation of people in development programmes and showed lack of respect for them in this respect. Implementation of programmes has been often marked by widespread public corruption and the functionaries have been reluctant to share information with the people. On the whole, they showed a lack of interest in development programmes and tended to implement them routinely and/or to distort them on the ground (Mehta, 1996a).

The Systemic Tendencies and the Items

The present questionnaire drew substantially from an earlier similar questionnaire which showed high construct validity and reliability (Mehta, 1989a: 75–88, 165–66). There was a tendency to justify even poor development performance, and a sense of complacency and unwillingness to utilise feedback in our development functionaries. Based on such earlier research, fieldwork and review studies, information about the observed behaviour of the functionaries was content-analysed and grouped into seven appropriate broad systemic tendencies. Such observed behaviours/ practices/tendencies, as seen in Table 5.4, formed the basis of the items for the present questionnaire.

Table 5.4
Systemic Tendencies in Development Functioning

1. **Caste-like cadre mentality:** attachment with one's own service/cadre; feelings of in-group and out-group; status consciousness.
2. **Tendency for centralisation:** reluctance to team with others and share power; unilateralism and working at cross-purposes; lack of linkages in functioning of programmes.
3. **Number and target syndrome:** non-responsiveness to people's needs and aspirations; lack of goal clarity; over-attention to number of activities and expenditure rather than quality and social impact.
4. **Reluctance (and resistance) to promoting people's participation:** lack of respect for people while implementing programmes; reluctance to involve people; reluctance to be accountable.
5. **Rentier-Dole syndrome:** programmes marked by widespread public corruption; reluctance to involve people; diverting public funds to personal advantage.
6. **Lack of interest in development:** tokenism: reluctance to implement policies; routine work without involvement; interest in lucrative posting rather than social development.
7. **Patronising manipulativeness:** behaving as patrons; unable to function as servants of people; promoting 'mai-baap' (paternalistic) tendency.

Source: Mehta (1989a, 1998: 61–66, Table 3.1)

After an initial tryout and critical examination, 21 statements were finally retained—three each for seven tendencies (Table 5.4). For instance, item 1 in the scale records that: 'There is a tendency among the public officials to concentrate more and more powers in their hands rather than to share power with their colleagues and subordinates'. The respondents were required to tick mark on a four-point scale, indicating either their strong agreement (1), or agreement (2), or disagreement (3), or strong disagreement (4), with the stated practice/tendency. The scale was, thus, designed to elicit response (attitude) to assessing some known systemic tendency (practice) in administrative behaviour in the functioning of our development programmes. The obtained responses would, in a way, show the respondents' readiness to evaluate known behaviours and aspects of development functioning on the ground. They may either defend the current development functioning (by disagreeing with the given statement) or show openness in this respect (by agreeing with the given statement). Greater the score, more defensive and favourable their attitude, and lower the score, more critical and flexible would be their attitude to assessing administrative behaviour and functioning of development programmes. The questionnaire was, thus, designed to yield information on respondents' readiness (or openness) to assessing administrative behaviour as well as to evaluating current development functioning.

Workplace Satisfaction (WPS Scale)

A workplace satisfaction questionnaire was included in the present study to understand the strength of the respondents' sense of integration vs. alienation at the workplace. The present questionnaire contains 24 items— six each for four dimensions of workplace satisfaction, namely, perceived influence, perceived amenities, perceived nature of job and perceived supervisory behaviour at the workplace. These four dimensions and the composite questionnaire have been found to be highly reliable and valid in earlier studies (Mehta, 1989a: 89–93).

Preliminary Critique and Tryout of the Instruments

Factor Analysis of the Preliminary Data

All these instruments were discussed in detail with experts in agricultural extension and researchers involved in rural and agricultural development with a view to edit, amend, delete and/or add items in the respective questionnaires. Wording of some items and sequencing of responses were modified as a result of such discussions. Instruments thus finalised were then tried out on a small group of agricultural extension researchers and officials in September 1995 who were then attending a training programme on motivation at New Delhi. They came from various institutes under the Indian Council for Agricultural Research (ICAR) and from agricultural universities and state departments of agricultural extension.

The Obtained Factors: Theoretical Validity and Reliability

The obtained responses were scored, as proposed, for 22 variables: seven dimensions of development functioning, four styles of leadership, four styles of development problem-solving, four measures of work satisfaction, and three measures of efficacy. The data thus derived was processed for principal component factor analysis which yielded seven rotated factors as seen in Table 5.5. These are briefly discussed as follows:

Table 5.5

Principal Component Factor Analysis of Preliminary Data **(N = 20)**

Rotated Factors (Varimax)	Eigen value	Per cent of Variance	Cumulative Percentage	h^2
1. Status quoism in development functioning	9.46	32.6	32.6	0.84
2. Dependency inducing–capability promoting (DIT–CPT) tendency	5.24	18.1	50.7	0.88
3. Workplace satisfaction (WPS)	3.36	12.5	63.2	0.85
4. Motivating-empowering leadership values/style (MOEM)	2.59	8.9	72.2	0.91
5. Sense of personal efficacy (SPE)	1.73	6.0	78.1	0.74
6. Patronising-educative leadership values/style (PAED)	1.59	5.5	83.6	0.85
7. Dominative leadership values/style (DOLS)	1.10	3.8	87.4	0.82

Factor 1: Development Functioning Attitude: status quoism (rigidity) vs. change proneness (flexibility).

All the seven dimensions included in the development functioning attitude questionnaire showed high positive loadings on Factor 1 (Appendix Table 5.1). Only one other variable, i.e., the facilitative style of dealing with development problems, showed significant negative loading on this factor. Obviously, the seven dimensions tended to show some common intervening factor impacting all of them. This was interpreted as status quoism (rigidity) vs. change proneness (flexibility) in approach to assessing administrative behaviour involved in development functioning. The data also suggested that those tending to disagree with the assessment that development functioning was characterised by certain dysfunctional systemic and behavioural tendencies, i.e., those who tended to be defensive in this regard, also tended to show low preference for 'facilitative' method of dealing with people's development problems. The intervening factor of status quoism explained substantial portion of the variance in each of the development functioning tendencies, suggesting high construct validity for the questionnaire which tended to work in the theoretically postulated manner.

Reliability of a measure is always either greater or at least equal to its communality (h^2) as obtained in factor analysis (Kerlinger, 1978: 665). High mean communality ($h^2 = 0.84$) as well as the high communalities for each of the seven dimensions, therefore, showed high reliability of the questionnaire for each measure of individual tendency and for the total instrument to measure the overall attitude to assessing administrative behaviour as reflected in development functioning (for further discussion of reliability and validity of this and other instruments, see Chapter 6). Higher the score, greater was the rigidity (status quoism), and lower the score, greater was the flexibility (change proneness) in accepting the presence of dysfunctional behavioural and systemic tendencies in development functioning. Thus, this common attitudnal factor seemed to intervene in the respondents' approach to assessing such development functioning tendencies.

Factor 2: Capability promoting vs. dependency inducing tendency (CPT–DIT) in dealing with development problems.
The four suggested styles of dealing with development problems, namely, 'directive', 'prescriptive', 'facilitative' and 'enabling' 'empowering', showed high loadings on Factor 2. Of these, the first three styles showed negative, and the fourth, i.e., the enabling style, showed high positive loadings. This factor was interpreted as the tendency to either promote capability or induce dependency in people while dealing with their development problems. Higher the tendency for promoting capability, lower was the tendency for inducing dependency and vice versa. Only one other variable, i.e., sense of initiative, showed significant positive loading on this factor. The results suggested, as could be expected, that the higher the tendency in development functionaries for promoting capability in people (while dealing with their development problems), the greater was their sense of initiative and autonomy. Here also, the instrument tended to work in the postulated direction showing high construct validity. It also showed high reliability as indicated by the average communality value on the four suggested styles ($h^2 = 0.88$). In fact, the enabling values/style used to interpret the factor showed very high reliability ($h^2 = 0.97$, see Appendix Table 5.2).

Factor 3: Workplace Satisfaction (WPS).

The four measures of workplace satisfaction, namely, satisfaction with perceived influence, amenities, nature of job and the supervisory behaviour at the workplace, showed high positive loadings on Factor 3 (Appendix Table 5.3). The findings here provided additional construct validity for the instrument which had shown similarly high validity in earlier studies (Mehta, 1989a: 93). Here also, the instrument showed very high reliability as indicated by the average communality ($h^2 = 0.85$). Three other variables, namely, prescriptive leadership values, directive style of dealing with development problems and the composite score on facilitative and enabling styles (labelled here as actor-promoting tendencies in dealing with development problems) also showed significant loadings (Appendix Table 5.3).

The negative loadings of prescriptive values and directive problem-solving, and the positive loading of empowering actor-promoting tendency in dealing with people's problems added further meaning to the factor of workplace satisfaction. Such satisfied people tended to show lower preference for prescriptive leadership values and the directive style of problem-solving, and greater tendency for promoting actor-like behaviour and capability in people while dealing with their problems. Leadership values and problem-solving tendencies, thus, emerged as important correlates of workplace satisfaction.

Factor 4: Motivating-Empowering leadership values/style (MOEM).

Three dimensions of leadership values/style, namely, directive, prescriptive and empowering/enabling showed higher loadings on this factor. Of these, the first two were negative and the third was a positive loading (Appendix Table 5.4). This factor was interpreted as motivating-empowering leadership values/style (MOEM) which seemed to be the opposite of dominative leadership values. One other variable, namely, sense of initiative and autonomy, showed significant positive loading on this factor adding further meaning to the interpretation. Greater the preference for such values or style, greater was the initiative and liking for autonomy at the workplace. Here again, sense of efficacy, particularly the sense of initiative, emerged as a significant positive correlate of motivating-empowering leadership values/style.

The questionnaire, on the whole, showed very high theoretical validity as well as reliability as indicated by the average communality for the four suggested sets of values ($h^2 = 0.87$). The measure of enabling/empowering leadership values/style by itself showed very high reliability ($h^2 = 0.91$). The leadership questionnaire, however, yielded two other factors thus suggesting a need for some revision in the scoring system, as discussed ahead.

Factor 5: Sense of Personal Efficacy (SPE).

The three measures of efficacy, namely, sense of initiative and autonomy, sense of self-esteem and sense of reflective thinking showed high positive loadings on Factor 5 (Appendix Table 5.5) which was interpreted as sense of personal efficacy. No other variable showed significant loading on this factor. The questionnaire was clearly working in the theoretically postulated direction yielding information on sense of personal efficacy. Besides high construct validity, the questionnaire also showed high reliability as indicated by the high average communality value ($h^2 = 0.74$) and by high communality values for each of the measures, particularly high for the first two measures and for the composite score.

Factor 6: Patronising-Educative leadership values/style (PAED).

The educative leadership value dimension of the questionnaire showed very high positive loading on Factor 6 with enabling leadership values/style showing high negative loading (Appendix Table 5.6). As discussed before, such a style valued 'educating' or coaching people while maintaining their recipient status and one's own patron status. The factor was, therefore, interpreted as patronising-educative leadership values/style which was quite different, maybe opposite of empowering leadership values/style which attached importance to initiative and actor behaviour in people (see Table 5.1). Interestingly, the perceived influence at the workplace showed significant loading on this factor. Greater the influence, greater was the preference for patronising leadership. High communality value for this dimension of leadership values ($h^2 = 0.85$) and high average communality value for the set of values included in the questionnaire ($h^2 = 0.87$) showed its high theoretical/construct validity as well as high reliability. It was an important theoretical finding, suggesting that leadership commonly described as 'facilitating' or 'educative' could have a rather disempowering impact on people.

Factor 7: Dominative Leadership values/styles (DOLS).

Preference for directive leadership values/style showed high positive loading on this factor. Interestingly, caste-like cadre mentality also showed significant positive loading on this factor (Appendix Table 5.7). Greater the preference for directive leadership values/style, greater was the disagreement with the evaluation that development functioning suffered from caste-like cadre mentality in administrative behaviour. In other words, those who tended to defend cadre-'service' system and the related status consciousness (and who, therefore, showed a strong sense of attachment or affinity with their cadre, if any) also showed greater preference for direct leadership values. Theoretically, it was an important finding that 'cadre mentality' was a very significant factor in dominative leadership. Although this variable showed significant negative loading on Factor 4, i.e., MOEM (Appendix Table 5.4), this emerged, also, as an independent factor interpreted here as dominative leadership values/styles (DOLS). This measure of directive leadership values showed high theoretical/construct validity as well as reliability ($h^2 = 0.82$), showing that the questionnaire was reliable in measuring preference for dominative leadership values/style.

Intervening Factors

The results of the factor analysis of the preliminary data showed high theoretical/construct validity and reliability for all the instruments. The instruments were, therefore, dependable for assessing preference for leadership values, tendencies in dealing with people's development problems, sense of workplace satisfaction, sense of personal efficacy and attitude to assessing development functioning. Such an attitude could be status quoist (or rigid or defensive), or change prone (open or flexible). Assured by the results of the preliminary factor analysis, the instruments were processed for further analyses and validation.

The validated questionnaires, as discussed earlier, were slightly revised in wording and sequencing of responses in some items. These were then administered to two further groups of agricultural extension scientists and officials. Group 1 consisted of 40 respondents, including nine women, of whom three were under 30 years of age, 17 between 30–40 years and 20 were above 40 years of age. Fourteen of such officials were drawn from various institutes under the ICAR and 26 from various agricultural universities, departments of agriculture and Krishi Vigyan Kendras (KVKs) in different states in the country. Most of these respondents held academic positions with doctoral degree to their credit. Group 2 also consisted of 40 respondents of whom only two were women; sixteen were between 30–40 years and rest above 40 years or age. Like group 1, majority of the respondents came from either some agricultural university, agricultural department or KVK and the remaining from the ICAR institutes.

These respondents had come to attend some training programme at New Delhi during 1995–96. The officials in group 1 attended a series of two training programmes, 20 each, on motivation. The respondents in Group 2 attended a series of two programmes, 20 each, on communication and audio-visual education. Group 1 checked the questionnaires, one at a time, at some interval during their training, while group 2 did so, in-between the training sessions or in their off-time after the training sessions.

Further Factor Analyses: Results

A total of 22 variables were included in the final instruments: seven in development functioning scale, four in leadership scale, four in problem-solving scale, three in efficacy scale and four in workplace scale. These were once again processed for principal component factor analysis, separately, for group 1, group 2 and the composite group. The factors thus derived from the data from each group are discussed as follows:

Factors Derived from Group 1

Factor analysis of the data obtained here yielded seven principal component factors (Appendix Table 5.8). These factors together accounted for 77 per cent of the variance in matrix obtained by the five given instruments. Four of the five instruments yielded one factor each, while the leadership values/style questionnaire yielded three. The latter were interpreted respectively as: prescriptive-dominative leadership values/style (Factor 4), dominative vs. empowering leadership value/style (Factor 5) and the patronising-educative leadership values/style (Factor 7). All the variables including the three leadership factors showed good average and/or individual communality values.

Interestingly, factors obtained here were the same as obtained from the preliminary data as reported earlier, with one important difference. In the earlier analysis, status quoism in development functioning accounted for as much as 33 per cent of the total variance in the matrix, while here it accounted for only 22 per cent. The communality values derived for each of the instruments/variables were also generally higher there as compared to the ones obtained here. Factors were, however, similar and interpreted as status quoism–change proneness (or rigidity-flexibility) in attitude to assessing development-functioning, workplace satisfaction, dependency inducing–capability promoting tendency in development problem-solving, sense of personal efficacy, and the three leadership factors.

Factors Derived from Group 2

The results of the factor analysis of data obtained from group 2 are seen in Appendix Table 5.9. Here also, the analysis yielded seven factors accounting for about 73 per cent of the variance in the matrix. There was, however, one important difference from group 1 and the analysis of the preliminary data. In the earlier two analyses, the development functioning attitude questionnaire yielded just one factor whereas here, it showed two factors, interpreted as status quoism vs. change proneness in development functioning (Factor 1) and defence of centralisation and cadre system in development functioning (Factor 3). On the other hand, the analyses here yielded only two leadership factors interpreted as dominative leadership vs. motivating-empowering leadership values/style (DOLS-MOEM) and the patronising-educative leadership values/style (PAED).

The Construct Variables: Factor Analysis of the Combined Scores

The total scores for group 1 for the constructs, as initially visualised and discussed before, were also processed for factor analysis. These constructs included dominative leadership (total of directive and prescriptive styles), integrative leadership (total of educative and enabling styles); pawn role inducing tendency (total of directive and prescriptive approach to problem-solving); actor role promoting tendency (total of facilitative and empowering approaches to problem-solving), total score on sense of efficacy, total development functioning score (total of seven tendencies) and the total workplace satisfaction score. The factor analysis of these seven constructs, as theoretically postulated (Appendix Table 5.10), accounted for 80 per cent of the variance in this matrix. These constructs showed only three common factors interpreted as: dependency inducing–capability promoting tendency in problem–solving (Factor 1), motivating-empowering leadership values/style (Factor 2) and status quoism vs. change proneness (or rigidity vs. flexibility) in assessing development functioning (Factor 3). Each of these factors also showed high mean commonality value. Interestingly, the problem-solving tendency emerged here as the most important factor, accounting for as much as 46 per cent of the total variance. On the whole, the results provided additional evidence of high construct validity and reliability of the concerned instruments.

The factor matrix, here, revealed some other interesting results. The sense of personal efficacy did not emerge as an independent factor but showed high loading on factor 1, i.e., capability promoting tendency (CPT), adding further meaning to this factor. Taking CPT as an independent variable, it explained as much as 52 per cent variance (square of factor loading of 0.720) in the sense of personal efficacy (SPE). These two, i.e., psychological empowerment (SPE) and capability are important goals of human development (Mehta, 1998: 102–28). It was noteworthy, therefore, that stronger the tendency in the development functionaries to promote capability in people while dealing with their problems, greater was their sense of efficacy. Further, the actor role promoting construct showed significant loading on Factor 2. MOEM explained 16 per cent variance (Factor loading = 0.405) in the actor role promoting tendency. Such significant relationship provided evidence for the hypothesis that democratic values enhance capability promoting behaviour in development functionaries. Further, this (MOEM) factor also explained 20 per cent variance in workplace satisfaction (factor loading = 0.443). Greater the preference for MOEM, greater was the WPS.

The workplace satisfaction, although, did not emerge as a distinct factor here, showed high loading (0.567) on the attitude of status quoism in development functioning. This factor thus explained as much as 32 per cent variance in workplace satisfaction. Greater the tendency for defending the current nature of development functioning, greater was the workplace satisfaction. Such association between the status quoist attitude in development functioning and workplace satisfaction was rather striking. This could help us understand the meaning of both the constructs. It was, thus, noteworthy that all the five theoretically postulated 'constructs' emerged as important in this analysis—three as independent and distinct factors, and two as meaningfully supportive variables. Although the number of variables in this analysis was small, it did seem to yield some useful insights. However, in view of some important differences in the results derived from the two groups, it was decided to pool all the data from the composite group and process it for principal factors in order to get a clearer picture.

Factor Analysis of the Data Obtained from the Composite Group

The composite results are seen in Table 5.6. The analysis yielded six factors which accounted for 64 per cent of the variance in the matrix. These factors were more or less the same as derived in the earlier analyses, yielding one factor each for development functioning (ADF), workplace satisfaction (WPS), development problem-solving (DPS) and sense of personal efficacy (SPE), and two leadership factors interpreted here as motivating-empowering leadership (MOEM) (vs. dominative-disempowering leadership) and patronising-educative leadership (PAED). The mean communality values derived for various instruments were generally lower here than the values obtained earlier. However, in view of the size and composite nature of the sample, factors derived were taken as final for further analyses. These factors were also common to all the factor analyses reported earlier, thus confirming their construct validity. The six obtained factors are briefly discussed as follows:

Table 5.6
Principal Component Analysis of the Data Obtained from Group 3
(Composite Group) **(N = 80)**

Rotated Factors (Varimax)	Eigen Value	Per cent of Variance	Cumulative Percentage	Mean h^2
1. Status quoism (vs. change-proneness) in development functioning (ADF)	3.55	16.1	16.1	0.58
2. Workplace satisfaction (WPS)	3.51	16.0	32.1	0.70
3. Dependency inducing vs. capability promoting tendency (DIT–CPT)	2.62	11.9	44.0	0.69
4. Sense of personal efficacy (SPE)	1.81	8.2	52.2	0.52
5. Motivating-empowering leadership (MOEM)	1.46	6.6	58.9	0.92
6. Patronising-educative leadership (PAED)	1.22	5.5	64.4	0.76

Status Quoism vs. Change Proneness (or Rigidity vs. Flexibility): Attitude to DF (DFA)

All the seven variables/systemic tendencies included in development functioning attitude (scale) except cadre mentality showed highly significant positive loadings on Factor 1 (Appendix Table 5.11). It was clear that there was an overall attitudinal pattern in the assessment of development functioning. This common factor, i.e. status quoism vs. change proneness, thus, played an important role in administrative-managerial behaviour.

It was interesting that none of the systemic tendencies showed significant correlation with approaches to dealing with development problems of the people nor with any of the leadership values/style. However, caste-like cadre mentality showed significant positive correlation with overall workplace satisfaction ($r = 0.296$, significant at 0.05 level), more particularly with the perceived influence at the workplace ($r = 0.312$, significant at 0.05 level). It appears that those who tended to favour the existing system of cadres in civil services and showed some kind of cadre mentality, i.e., those who tended to be status quoist or rigid in this respect, were rewarded by the system. They tended to enjoy greater influence at the workplace. Stronger the status quoism and defensive behaviour in this respect (i.e., the cadre mentality), greater was the perceived influence at the workplace and greater was their overall workplace satisfaction. As discussed ahead, cadre mentality (as indicated by the status quoist attitude to this tendency in DF) showed a significant loading on workplace satisfaction. We would examine the significance of cadre mentality further while discussing results of the multiple regression and analysis of variance in Chapter 6.

Workplace Satisfaction (WPS)

All the four variables of workplace satisfaction showed very high positive loadings on Factor 2 (Appendix Table 5.12). It was clearly a factor of workplace satisfaction vs. alienation, showing high construct validity for this measure. Interestingly, cadre mentality also showed significant positive loading on this factor. It explained 12 per cent variance in the dependent variable of cadre mentality. This result further confirmed the positive correlation between the two variables as reported earlier. It also showed that cadre mentality was somewhat different from the other tendencies assessed for development functioning, as discussed before. It was thus interesting that the functionaries, in this case the agricultural extension scientists and officials, who felt satisfied and integrated at their workplace also tended more to defend the cadre system and to deny that the related status consciousness marred the management and functioning of development. In other words, greater the satisfaction and integration at the workplace, greater was their sense of belonging and the tendency to defend their cadre. Thus, workplace (i.e., the structure and policies of the workplace) seemed to emerge as an important factor in inculcating a sense of cadre-belonging and satisfaction in this regard.

Dependency Inducing vs. Capability Promoting Tendency in Problem-solving (DIT – CPT)

All the four approaches or styles (namely, directive, prescriptive, educative and empowering) of dealing with development problems showed high loading on this factor (Appendix Table 5.13). Those who tended to deny, that our development functioning suffered from centralisation also showed significant negative loading on this factor of CPT. Thus, those who tended to promote empowerment and capability in people also, showed a greater need for decentralisation in order to improve the management and functioning of development.

This factor in problem-solving was bipolar. The first three variables seemed to work in one direction and the fourth, i.e., the empowering style, in the opposite direction. As discussed earlier, the first three styles indicate routine-directive, officious, status-oriented and coaching-educative approaches to dealing with development and other problems of the people in which the functionary remained the 'patron' and the people, the 'recipients'. On the other hand, the empowering style seeks to develop an actor role in the people—making them the 'subjects' by helping them move away from being the 'objects' of development. This factor was, thus, interpreted and confirmed as dependency inducing vs. capability promoting tendency (DIT–CPT) in dealing with people's problems.

Although efficacy variables did not show significant loadings on this factor, sense of initiative and autonomy as well as the combined sense of efficacy showed significant negative correlations ($r = 0.260$ and $r = 0.342$ respectively, both significant at 0.05 level) with directive style of problem-solving. The results seemed to suggest that the functionaries with greater tendency to induce dependency among the people, tended to show lower sense of initiative as well as lower sense of efficacy (or greater sense of powerlessness). Alternatively, greater the tendency to promote capability among the people and to inculcate in them an actor role, greater too was the initiative and sense of efficacy. These correlations were in line with the results of factor analysis of the composite constructs (see Appendix Table 5.10) as discussed before. The correlational analysis also showed another interesting indication. The greater the tendency to induce dependency in people while dealing with development problems, the greater also was the tendency to be dissatisfied with the supervisory behaviour at the workplace (or between directive problem-solving and supervisory behaviour was –0.293, significant at 0.05 level). May be, the dependency inducing behaviour of the superiors at the workplace, on the one hand was replicated by 'subordinate' functionaries, on the other hand, with the people on the ground level, while dealing with their developmental problems. In other words, it could also be said that greater the satisfaction in superior-subordinate relationship at the workplace, greater was the tendency in the subordinate functionaries to promote capability in people. The results seemed to suggest relationship between some aspects of workplace management and some aspects of development management, including the functionaries' development problem-solving behaviour. We examine such relationships further in Chapter 6.

Sense of Personal Efficacy (SPE)

Initiative, self-esteem and reflective action showed high positive loadings on Factor 4 (Appendix Table 5.14). The directive leadership values/style and the dependency inducing tendency (constituted by directive and prescriptive style of problem-solving) showed significant negative loadings on this factor. Thus, greater the sense of personal efficacy, lower was the preference for directive leadership values and also, for dependency inducing tendency in dealing with people's problems. Sense of personal efficacy seemed to explain 22 per cent variance in directive (or dominative) leadership values and 21 per cent and 9 per cent variance respectively, in the two variables of the dependency inducing tendency. These results were similar to the findings derived from the factor analysis of the constructs (see Appendix Table 5.10) discussed earlier. From both theoretical and practical points of view, these were important findings which seemed to show that efficacious people were likely to be more motivating and empowering in their leadership values and also, that they would tend more to promote capability and inculcate actor behaviour in people while dealing with their development and other problems. The findings here, thus, provided empirical support to conceptualisation of the changing political behaviour, as discussed in Chapter 1, that greater the sense of personal efficacy, lower was the tendency to feel threatened by the actor role and capability of the people, and also, greater was their commitment to egalitarian and democratic values.

Motivating-Empowering vs. Dominative-Disempowering Leadership Values/Styles

Variables of leadership scale, namely, directive, prescriptive and enabling values/styles showed significant loadings on Factor 5 (Appendix Table 5.15—the first two showed positive, and the third, i.e., enabling style, showed very negative loading). The educative leadership values/style showed no loading on this factor. Also, no other variable showed significant loading on this factor. This factor was identified as bipolar leadership values/style, namely, directive-disempowering vs. motivating-empowering leadership values/style.

Interestingly, the correlational analysis showed a significant positive correlation between the functionaries' age ($r = 0.266$, significant at 0.05 level) and directive leadership values/style. It (the dominative-authoritarian values) also showed positive correlation with pawn-inducing tendency in problem-solving ($r = 0.33$, significant at 0.05 level) and negative correlation with actor-promoting tendency ($r = -0.307$, significant at 0.05 level). Interestingly, greater the preference for the enabling leadership style (i.e., egalitarian democratic leadership values), greater was the tendency to promote an actor role, i.e., capability ($r = 0.329$, significant at 0.05 level), while greater the dominative leadership values/style, greater was the tendency to induce the pawn role, i.e., dependency ($r = 0.293$, significant at 0.05 level), and lower was the tendency to promote capability among people while dealing with their problems ($r = 0.293$, significant at 0.05 level).

Patronising–Educative Leadership Values/Styles (PAED)

The educative leadership values/style showed high positive loading on Factor 6 while prescriptive as well as enabling leadership values/style showed significant negative loadings on this factor, as seen in Appendix Table 5.16. The prescriptive approach to development problem-solving and the cadre mentality also, showed significant positive loadings on this factor. This factor was obviously distinct from Factor 5 which was interpreted as motivating-empowering leadership values/style (MOEM). It seemed to be the opposite of the directive style of leadership. This factor, therefore, appeared to be neither directive nor empowering. It was, however, interesting that this factor was associated with the prescriptive approach to development problem-solving and also, with cadre mentality. It explained 15 per cent variance in the latter and 7 per cent variance in the former. Greater the preference for PAED, greater was the tendency to prescribe, i.e., to reinforce dependency in dealing with people's problems, and also, greater was the defence of the cadre system and status consciousness. This factor of leadership behaviour was informed by 'patronising' and 'educative' or 'coaching' values. This was, accordingly, interpreted as patronising-educative leadership values/style (PAED). Maybe, this factor was informed by a preference for just depositing some information in the minds of people perceived as 'subordinates'. Such a narrative and 'banking' system of education is designed to subjugate the learners—the people (Freire, 1972: 57–74), where some data or slogans is mechanically used without really developing the people's reasoning power or capability (Table 5.1). No wonder, such values promoted prescriptive development problem-solving which, in turn, tended to reinforce (and satisfy) the need for status in the development functionaries (see Chapter 1 for exclusionary communication in development programmes).

To sum up: a total of 22 variables—four for leadership, four for problem-solving, three for efficacy, seven for development functioning and four for workplace satisfaction, yielded six principal components (factors). These were interpreted as: attitude of status quoism vs. change proneness (or rigidity vs. flexibility) in development functioning (ADF), workplace satisfaction (WPS), dependency inducing vs. capability promoting tendency (DIT–CPT) in development (or workplace) problem-solving, sense of personal efficacy (SPE), motivating-empowering leadership values/style (MOEM) and patronising-educative leadership values/style (PAED). We discuss some conceptual models to explain behaviours and their implications for workplace, development and democratisation in the next chapter.

Trends in and Contributors to Development-related Behaviour

Reliability and Validity of the Instruments: The Behavioural Trends

Appendix Tables 6.1 to 6.6 show standard errors of the mean scores obtained by development officials, in this case, the agricultural extension scientists/officials. The mean scores indicate tendencies in the concerned development functionaries with regard to: leadership styles, problem-solving behaviour, sense of personal efficacy, attitude to development functioning, workplace satisfaction and the needs for personal achievement, social achievement and influence. The standard errors for all individual and composite mean scores, as seen in the tables earlier, were uniformly low suggesting that the obtained statistics indicated such behavioural tendencies in the given universe of the development functionaries, i.e., agricultural scientists and officials drawn from the various institutes of the ICAR, agricultural universities in various states and other institutes/agencies of agricultural extension. The low standard errors also indicated high reliability of the obtained mean scores for all the instruments under report here.

Leadership Styles and Problem-solving Behaviour

The data showed that the concerned development officials, on the whole, tended to prefer egalitarian and democratic values as represented in the enabling style (MOEM) more than the authoritarian values or the patronising educating values as represented respectively, in the dominative and patronising leadership styles. The data also showed lower preference for using dependency inducing problem-solving than its opposite, the capability promoting problem-solving behaviour. As such data indicated trends in the given population of development functionaries, theoretically, it was important that the agricultural extension scientists and officials thought more of the motivating and capability promoting problem-solving approach.

Sense of Personal Efficacy, Workplace Satisfaction and Attitude to Development Functioning

The given development officials also showed somewhat higher than average sense of personal efficacy and, relatively speaking, somewhat lower sense of initiative and reflective thinking than self-esteem. They also tended to show somewhat higher than average overall work satisfaction. Relatively, they were more positive about the nature of their job and also about their supervisors' behaviour than about their influence and participation, and amenities available to them at their workplace. Thus, they showed some sense of dissatisfaction with the welfare and participatory situations at their workplace and interestingly also with the functioning of our development programmes. This was particularly important in view of the fact that the concerned development officials were involved either in conducting research and/or in actually implementing field programmes relating to rural and agricultural development.

Motivational Needs

In addition to the instruments mentioned here, the development functionaries also provided data on the strength of their three motivational needs, namely, the need for personal achievement, need for social achievement and need for influence.[1] They tended to show comparatively higher need for personal achievement than the other two needs. The low standard errors of the obtained mean scores (see Appendix Table 6.6) showed that such trends were indicative of the tendencies in the given population of the development functionaries. On the whole, they tended to think more in terms of personal excellence and quality, in their work and maybe in life, than similar excellence and quality in group/collective work and/ or in social life. It was interesting that their need for influence was not that strong, although, as extension officials, it is very much a part of their function to influence farmers. It was also interesting that they did not think so much of social achievement though, being extension functionaries and scientists, they were very much concerned with improving farming and other such collective performance.

To sum up: in addition to the need for personal achievement, the concerned development officials were inclined to prefer motivating empowering leadership values and capability promoting approach to dealing with people's development needs and problems. Relatively speaking, they showed less initiative and greater self-esteem. They also tended to be critical of the functioning of development programmes on the ground level. Though they perceived challenge in their jobs, they showed a lurking sense of dissatisfaction with their service and working conditions as well as with the influence and participation available to them at their workplace.

Trends Obtained for Managers and Workers

The instruments mentioned earlier yielded some interesting results from junior to middle-evel managers and skilled and semi-skilled workers at a state-run mines and minerals enterprise.[2]

Standard errors of the obtained mean scores were also uniformly low here showing their high reliability in predicting these behavioural tendencies in the larger population of managers and workers in similar mines and mineral enterprises.

The concerned managers and workers tended to think more of influence than of personal achievement and much less of social achievement. It was, thus, interesting that such mines and minerals' personnel thought much more of personal accomplishment than of collective achievements although their work was quite interrelated with each other. Interestingly, such trends were validated by the 'knowledge' articulated by the senior management personnel, the trade union functionaries as well as by the middle managers and the workmen themselves while discussing and identifying the strengths and weaknesses/needs of the organisation. It was an interesting finding that managers were relatively weak on the need for influence and the workers, on the concern for collective achievement. At the same time, the population under report here, i.e., the managers and workers, perceived amenities, nature of their job and the supervisory behaviour/practices with somewhat greater satisfaction than the influence and participation available to them at their workplace and in the organisation.

As discussed earlier (Chapter 5), influence and participation was indicated by the perceived availability of information and information sharing, involvement in decision-making concerning matters of their interest and welfare, mechanism for grievance handling, participation in work planning, listening from others in the organisation and freedom to express difference of opinion with their superiors. The perceived amenities included: fringe benefits like medical facilities, salary and other such composition, availability of drinking water and canteen, recreation and housing facilities. The nature of job indicated perceptions regarding opportunity to learn new work, to use skills and abilities, to enjoy freedom on the job and the significance and social worthwhileness of their work. Supervisory behaviour/practices included perception of superior-subordinate relationship, respect given to their suggestions, appreciation of good work, superiors' image of their capability, planning of work in organisation and support available to them from their superiors. It was, thus, noteworthy that relatively speaking, the workmen and the executives were somewhat more satisfied with the situation obtaining with regard to their supervisors' behaviours and practices. One interesting finding here was that despite the satisfaction with the incentive scheme and other amenities, both the workmen and the managers were not clearly satisfied in this regard. They talked about the need for improving the quality of such facilities. They also thought that the incentive scheme put over-emphasis on quantity at the cost of quality. Incidentally, the statistical findings here were clearly corroborated by the knowledge generated by the senior managers in individual interviews as well as by the junior managers and the workmen themselves, in small group discussions, independently of the questionnaires.

Leadership Values and Styles

The workmen and the managers showed some preference for motivating and empowering values. However, the dominative and the paternalistic values also attracted substantial attention. In fact, the combination of these two was higher than the tendency for the motivating-empowering style. On the whole, therefore, the tendency for dominative and paternalistic values was more powerful. As conceptualised in Table 5.1, such values could contribute to a tendency for directing and stimulating the workforce for extracting work by various methods. This could, therefore, weaken the employees' intrinsic motivation for seeking challenging goals of creativity and higher production.

The leadership styles were further reflected in their problem-solving behaviour. While there was a substantial tendency for promoting capability in workmen and others, there was, at the same time, an equally strong tendency for inducing dependency. Taking the two together, i.e., the leadership values and the problem-solving behaviour, there was, thus, a considerable tendency for dominative leadership and dependency inducing problem-solving behaviour in the organisation.

Sense of Personal Efficacy

The findings here showed a substantial sense of self-esteem and a tendency for reflective thinking and reasoning in the organisation. However, the sense of initiative was relatively lower. The lack of good sense of initiative was likely to hamper creative efforts in the organisation. It was further interesting that the efficacy perceived by the managers and workmen for others in the organisation was uniformly lower than, not only their own sense of initiative but also, the overall sense of efficacy. On the whole, the population under study seemed to think that the members of the organisation were weak on initiative and only slightly above average on other dimensions of efficacy. They were not very positive about capability of their work group in the organisation. The data, thus, clearly showed that the members perceived lack or low sense of initiative in the organisation.

Another study, conducted on Iranian managers working in the mineral and mining sector of public sector steel industry (Reza, 1999), also found very low standard errors for the obtained mean scores of the individual dimensions of leadership behaviour and the perceived conditions of work. It also showed low standard errors for the obtained mean scores on motivational needs, namely, the need for personal achievement, need for social achievement and the need for influence. This study separately found Spearman-Browen reliability of 0.71 for the leadership questionnaire and 0.71 for the work questionnaire.

Thus, besides high reliability of mean scores and high construct validity for the various instruments as found in factor analysis (see Appendix Tables 5.1 to 5.16), the managers and workmen at this state enterprise for mines and minerals provided a striking cross-validation between the data obtained on the various questionnaires and the knowledge generated by the senior managers in individual interviews and the present managers and workmen in separate small group discussions (Mehta, 1999).

Contributors to the Variance in Development Behaviours

A stepwise multiple regression analysis of the data obtained from development functionaries/officials identified some significant contributors to the variance in case of each of the behaviours mentioned before.[3] Some 32 variables (see Appendix Table 6.7) including three background variables, six leadership behaviour variables, six problem-solving behaviour variables, four variables on efficacy, eight variables of development functioning and five variables of workplace satisfaction were processed for this analysis. The results are briefly discussed as follows.

Problem–solving Behaviour

Directive Approach to Development Problem–solving

The perceived supervisory behaviour at the workplace, the attitude to the Rentier-Dole tendency in development functioning and the sense of reflective efficacy emerged as significant correlates of directive approach to problem-solving. These together explained 23 per cent of variance in this tendency (the adjusted variance for the population was 0.20 in this respect, see Appendix Table 6.8). It was interesting that dissatisfaction with supervisory behaviour or alienation on this count at the workplace emerged as the most important independent variable in this respect. Greater the functionaries' positive perception of their supervisors at the workplace, lower was the directive tendency (i.e., dependency inducing tendency) in them for dealing with development problems. The superior-subordinate relationship at the workplace, thus, emerged as a very important factor in functionaries' development (problem-solving) behaviour on the ground. It indicated that such 'alienated' functionaries tended to be more authoritarian while dealing with people's needs and problems. They probably tended to replicate their bosses' behaviour with them with people treating them as their subordinates. Further, lower the functionaries' sense of reflective efficacy, greater was their tendency for directive approach to development problems. The sense of reflective efficacy is informed by a self-image of quality and challenge-seeking 'actor' role (see Table 5.3). Development functionaries having such efficacy were much less inclined to use dependency inducing practices while working with people. Thus, both from the theoretical as well as from the management's point of view, it was a very important finding.

On the other hand, the functionaries' status quoist attitude, as indicated by their reluctance to accept that there was a Rentier-Dole tendency in our development functioning, was a significant positive contributor to their tendency for directive problem-solving. It was interesting that functionaries, comfortable with the Rentier-Dole phenomenon in our administrative and political behaviour, also showed greater tendency to inducing dependency (a kind of Dole behaviour) in people. In fact, the two, i.e., the Rentier-Dole and the dependency inducing tendencies, were like two sides of the same coin. It was, therefore, of great practical significance that the Rentier-Dole phenomenon (public corruption) which is being increasingly debated as a public issue of great national importance, tended to thrive by contributing to the inducement of dependency and 'pawn-' like behaviour in people. Perhaps the corrupt functionaries, whether bureaucratic or political, realise that the Rentier-Dole 'business' can continue only as long as people continue to harbour their traditional sense of dependency. It was, therefore, only expected that such functionaries would use dependency inducing directive approach to development problem-solving. It was also noteworthy, though ironical, that such (i.e., dependency inducing) development functionaries enjoyed greater influence at their workplace. Greater the perceived influence at the workplace, (theoretically may be, greater the seniority and higher the office), greater was the tendency to induce dependency in people while dealing with development problems.

It was, thus, interesting that the dependency inducing type of development functionaries were not happy with their superiors at the workplace. At the same time, they were reluctant to seeking challenge and quality in their performance and for taking an 'actor-' role, thus, themselves showing a sense of dependency. They, however, felt quite influential at their workplace. They probably used such influence to replicating dependency in their own subordinates and in people, while implementing development programmes. Such superior-subordinate relationships are typical of a bureaucratic hierarchical organisation and work culture where the subordinates feel unhappy with their superiors' behaviour but, in turn, replicate similar behaviour with their own subordinates and people on the ground.

Prescriptive Development Problem-solving

The motivating-empowering leadership values/style (MOEM) emerged as the most important factor in explaining variance in the prescriptive development problem-solving behaviour. The second most important variable was the perceived nature of job at the workplace. These two variables together explained 13 per cent of the variance in the dependent variable (adjusted $R = 0.11$, $F = 5.89$, significant at 0.004 level). The prescriptive problem-solving represented an 'officious' and status-related bureaucratic approach to dealing with people's problems. It was another important element in the tendency to induce dependency in people.

It was significant that lower the extension officials' preference for egalitarian and democratic values represented in MOEM, greater was the tendency in them to prescribe and to induce dependency in people. In other words, lower the preference for MOEM in the development functionaries, greater would be the tendency in them to induce dependency in people. It was also interesting that out of the four work-related measures, only challenge, meaningfulness and variety as perceived in the job content emerged as a significant contributor to the prescriptive problem-solving behaviour. In other words, greater the job satisfaction at the workplace, greater was the prescriptive tendency in development functionaries.

Thus, the development functionaries, given to prescriptive problem-solving, showed positive perception of their job but were weak on egalitarian motivational empowering values. Job satisfaction, however, showed neither linear nor non-linear relationship with leadership values (Appendix Table 6.9). Such satisfaction was therefore value neutral. This suggested that job satisfaction, although important, was not instrumental in denting the traditional dependency inducing behaviour in development functionaries. On the contrary, it could even boost prescriptive behaviour, particularly when egalitarian and motivational values are weak.

Facilitative Problem-solving

Gender was the only significant independent variable which explained about 9 per cent variance in the tendency for facilitative-educative problem-solving. Adjusting it for the population (i.e., the agricultural extension scientists and officials), it explained about 8 per cent variance in this tendency (F = 7.6, significant at 0.007 level). Thus, the male agricultural scientists and extension officials (the indicative code here was 1 for males and 2 for females) showed much greater tendency for facilitative problem-solving than the female officials. They seemed to be supportive but not so much empowering in their development behaviour. Though they tended to 'help' people, they were reluctant to yield the 'actor' space to them. It was also interesting that neither the dominative leadership values (DOLS) nor the motivating-empowering values (MOEM) made any significant contribution to the variance in this approach. Thus, this tendency was neither clearly dominative nor clearly empowering. It needs to be recalled here that this kind of development problem-solving showed high positive loading on the factor of dependency inducing tendency (DIT). In fact, it showed much higher loading than directive and prescriptive approaches (see Appendix Table 5.13). Thus, though it was somewhat different from both the directive and prescriptive approaches, the same common intervening factor (DIT) impacted this approach also.

Enabling Problem-solving Behaviour

Interestingly, dominative leadership values/style (DOLS) emerged as the only significant negative predictor of enabling problem-solving behaviour. Thus, weaker the dominative-inegalitarian values, stronger was the preference among the development functionaries for promoting capability in people while dealing with their various problems. Factor analysis showed (Chapter 5) the dominative vs. empowering values as a bipolar factor. Also, in the given response scale, lower the dominative score, higher was the empowering score and vice versa. The present development officials tended to show relatively lower preference for DOLS (see Appendix Table 6.1) and greater tendency to promote capability in people (Appendix Table 6.2). However, despite the low mean score on DOLS, it was clear that it worked as a powerful weakener of capability promoting practices in our development programmes. May be, such leadership values have contributed to poor human development in the country. The results here indicated that democratic and egalitarian values (opposite of dominative and authoritarian leadership values) weakened the prescriptive, and significantly boosted the capability promoting development behaviour.

Among the several independent variables included in the present study, only MOEM was found to explain 7 to 8 per cent of the variance in capability promoting tendency. There was, thus, a need to address future research to identify other factors which could contribute to promotion and strengthening of capability and empowerment promoting behaviour in government and non-government development functionaries. This was critically important for augmenting social and economic achievements of the country.

Capability Promoting Development Behaviour

The four variables of development problem-solving, namely, directive, prescriptive, facilitative and enabling, showed loadings on a common intervening factor of dependency inducing–capability promoting tendency (Chapter 5; Appendix Table 5.2). As discussed earlier, these four responses were converted into a four-point scale from 1 to 4 in order to obtain an overall score on a composite capability promoting tendency (CPT). As in the case of enabling approach, the stepwise multiple regression analysis showed only one significant negative correlate—the dominative leadership values/style (DOLS), which accounted for as much as 10 per cent of the variance in CPT. There was, thus, no doubt that lower the preference for dominative-inegalitarian leadership values, greater was the tendency in the functionaries to promote capability in people.

The sense of self-esteem and the reluctance to promote people's participation in development also emerged as important predictors although, statistically, not clearly significant. These independent variables were, however, psychologically important. The greater the sense of self-esteem, which included self-image of innovativeness, risk-taking and a sense of self-worth, the greater was the tendency for capability promoting development behaviour. This was supported by the earlier finding where sense of personal efficacy (SPE) showed a very high loading on the tendency to promote capability (Appendix Table 5.10). In turn, SPE explained considerable variance in the preference for directive leadership values and in the tendency to induce dependency vs. promote capability in people (Appendix Table 5.14). In addition to the sense of self-esteem, it was meaningful that greater the positive attitude to promoting people's participation in development, stronger was the functionaries' tendency to promote capability in people.

Leadership Values/Styles:
Sense of Personal Efficacy and Work Satisfaction

Three leadership values/styles, namely dominative leadership values (DOLS—combination of directive and prescriptive styles), paternalistic-educative values (PAED) and motivating-empowering values (MOEM) showed several significant contributors to their variance. The results (reported in Appendix Tables 6.9) are briefly discussed as follows:

Dominative Leadership (DOLS)

Capability promoting development behaviour was the most important negative contributor to DOLS. The employer was the next important predictor, (the code was 1 for those employed at the state level and 2 for those employed at some ICAR institute). These two clearly significant contributors accounted for about 15 per cent of the variance in DOLS. Two other independent variables, namely, the age and the welfare at the workplace also emerged near about significant correlates. Thus, older the functionaries, greater was the preference for dominative leadership values. The perceived work amenities were a negative contributor. Greater the satisfaction with working conditions, lower was the preference for DOLS.

The employer represented the importance of the conditions of work including service and working conditions. It was no wonder that when the employer was held constant, lower the perceived work amenities, greater was the tendency for DOLS. The findings here were, therefore, important from the practical point of view. Satisfactory employment and working conditions, and planned efforts at training and education could help prepare the functionaries to promote capability in people which, in turn, could accelerate the pace of our social and economic progress.

Patronising-Educative Leadership (PAED)

It was interesting that gender emerged as the only and the most important factor in the patronising-educative leadership values. Unlike the problem-solving behaviour, where male functionaries showed significantly greater inclination for facilitative-educative approach, here, females tended to show significantly greater preference for PAED. It was also noteworthy that employer emerged as somewhat significant correlate of PAED. It was interesting that the agricultural extension scientists and officials employed at the ICAR were more patronising than those employed at the state-level organisations. As the female functionaries were more patronising in their values than males, does it mean that such values carry an element of patronising nurturance? Such values were informed by preference for banking system of education and by cadre mentality. Such leadership values were neither dominative nor empowering (Chapter 5). In our centralised system of development functioning, those working at the central level, such as those employed at the ICAR, tended to set norms of functioning elsewhere in the country. In such a situation, the ICAR functionaries motivated by patronising values could release trend-setting behaviours in the system.

Motivating-Empowering Leadership (MOEM)

The prescriptive development problem-solving emerged here as the most important negative predictor of MOEM. Interestingly, and in contrast to DOLS, welfare satisfaction was a significant positive predictor of motivating-empowering leadership. Greater the satisfaction with work amenities and conditions of work, greater was the preference for the motivating-empowering leadership values (MOEM).

It was noteworthy that greater the need for influence, lower was the preference for MOEM. It was not clear whether it was a need for authoritarian influence, as it did not show any separate relationship with DOLS. It was, however, certainly not egalitarian and empowering in nature. As development officials exercise influence over the poor, it was quite likely that they used it in an authoritarian way. It could be particularly so with those having high need for influence. It was supported by the fact that 'prescriptive' ones tended to show lower preference for empowering leadership.

It was, thus, clear that perceived work amenities, prescriptive problem-solving behaviour and the need for influence were important correlates of such empowering values among the development functionaries. While the prescriptive tendency and the need for influence dented and weakened democratic-empowering values, interestingly, welfare at the workplace boosted them. The work organisation, i.e., the conditions of work, particularly the supervisory behaviour and work amenities, thus, emerged as very important factor in shaping empowering democratic leadership values on the one hand, and in weakening the traditional dependency inducing development behaviour, on the other.

Sense of Personal Efficacy (SPE)

The directive approach to development problem-solving and the age of the respondent emerged as significant correlates of the sense of personal efficacy (Appendix Table 6.10). These two independent variables together explained 19 per cent of the variance in the SPE (reduced to 17 per cent when adjusted for population). These findings assumed greater significance in view of the fact that the sense of reflective efficacy weakened the directive approach to problem-solving and the sense of self-esteem boosted capability promoting behaviour (Appendix Table 6.8). Also, the older development functionaries were found to show greater preference for dominative leadership (Appendix Table 6.9).

Taken together, the present study indicated that inculcation and reinforcement of SPE (positive self-concept) among development functionaries could weaken the traditional dependency for inducing behaviour (designed to inducing negative self-concept in people). In other words, psychological empowerment of the development functionaries could replicate similar empowerment among the people for whom they are supposed to work.

Workplace Satisfaction

The caste-like cadre mentality emerged as the only significant correlate of workplace satisfaction. It explained some 9 per cent of its variance (adjusted variance for the population was 8 per cent, Appendix Table 6.10).

There was a very significant linear relationship between workplace satisfaction and caste-like cadre mentality. It seems that greater the psychological attachment with the 'cadre' or 'service' and greater the status consciousness and satisfaction in this regard, greater was the development functionaries' work satisfaction. The two seemed to work as reciprocal reinforcers in this respect. The 'cadrely'-oriented were more integrated with their workplace and vice versa. It was interesting that this important systemic factor carried vitally important psychological spinoffs. By implication, the same system left out a large number of key functionaries, i.e., those who were critical of such a caste-like system in administration, with great dissatisfaction.

The Motivational Needs

Importance of the employer, as discussed earlier, was further established by its emergence as the most significant factor in the members' need for personal achievement (see Appendix Table 6.11). As the employer represents availability of working and service conditions, the finding here suggested the importance of the objective conditions of work and the members' perception of such conditions. However, it may also indicate availability of better reward and work system. It was, therefore interesting that the objective condition of work was such an important factor in releasing concern for excellence and better performance in the members. In this particular case, the development functionaries drawn from institutes under the ICAR showed much greater concern for excellence than those working at some state-level organisation. Interestingly, the concern for influence and power significantly weakened the concern for excellence. The greater the craving for influence, the lower was this concern. On the other hand, greater the interest in development functioning (i.e., lower the tokenism), greater was the need for social or collective achievement. Interestingly, the tendency for centralisation in development functioning and, by implication, in administration was also a significant correlate of this need. It was very significant, however, that the concern for social goals of development and for collective achievement of such goals was accompanied significantly by interest in proper implementation of such programmes. Those who were not interested were also not motivated by such social goals.

Motivating-empowering leadership values emerged as a very important significant factor in the need for influence. Greater the tendency for using motivating-empowering and democratic values, lower was the concern for influence and power. In this sense, the need for influence here was associated more with dominative leadership values. It was, therefore, not surprising that those showing greater need for influence were also least concerned with excellence and quality in performance. This finding was important in view of the unequal social organisation and the history of dominative and exclusionary communication in development (see Chapter 1).

Workplace and Development Functioning

None of the independent variables included in the study met the criteria for entry into the equation for multiple regression analysis of the assessment of development functioning. It was noteworthy that independent variables pertaining to leadership values, development problem-solving behaviour, workplace satisfaction and sense of personal efficacy showed no linear relationship with such assessment. As discussed earlier, present function-aries were critical of the nature of development functioning and the related administrative behaviour. The findings here showed that, such an assess-ment was widespread irrespective of other variables. They probably thought that such tendencies (see Table 5.4) permeated the entire system of administration and government functioning.

Low and High Status Quoism in Development Functioning: Non-Linear Relationship

In view of these results and in view of the importance of development practice, i.e., development functioning, the matter was further pursued. Some significant results (seen in Appendix Tables 6.12 to 6.17) are briefly discussed as follows.

The 'Low' and 'High' Groups

As discussed earlier, the agricultural extension scientists and officials were, on the whole, critical (i.e., showing low status quoism) of our development functioning (see Appendix Table 6.4). When divided as high and low on status quoism, though they differed very significantly in their mean scores (see Table 6.1), qualitatively, all of them tended to agree—the low more than the high group—that our programme implementation was dysfunctional (theoretically, a score of two on a four-point scale, i.e., a score of 42 or less on 21 items, represents an 'agree' response and a score of 63 or more represents 'disagree').

Table 6.1
Mean Scores on Status Quoism in Development Functioning of the 'Low' and 'High' Groups

		N	Mean Score	SD	SE
Group 1	Low	34	36.59	4.98	0.854
Group 2	High	46	46.54	6.20	0.914

Notes: For pooled variance estimate, t value = –5.11, P = 0.000.
For separate variance estimate, t value = –5.06, P = 0.00.

Though both the groups were critical of development functioning, the 'Low' group showed lower mean scores on all the given tendencies (the difference in the mean scores for the two groups was statistically significant at 0.000 level in all the tendencies). This group was, thus, consistently more critical (see Table 5.4 for DF variables and tendencies) than the 'High' group. These results thus confirmed the findings of factor analysis (Chapter 5) that the variances in assessment of all the seven administrative tendencies were impacted by a common intervening factor which was designated as an attitude of status quoism in development functioning.

No Significant Difference by Independent Variables

The lack of relationship between status quoism (or assessment of development functioning) and some important independent behavioural variables was confirmed when the high and the low groups showed no mean difference in this respect. Thus, the attitude of status quoism in development functioning did not seem to be related, even non-linearly, to leadership behaviour, sense of personal efficacy, workplace satisfaction and to individual psychological needs of personal achievement, social achievement and influence in a significant way. The results here, thus, provided strong evidence that the agricultural scientists and officials (all of them experts) were critical of the nature of development functioning, irrespective of their other psychological differences.

Though there was no significant statistical difference by other variables, the results did seem to suggest some interesting trends. Relatively speaking, those (of the agricultural extension scientists and officials) with greater status quoist attitude, i.e., low change proneness, tended to perceive greater amenities at their workplace and tended to show greater preference for prescriptive problem-solving. Such status quoist officials also seemed to be motivated more by the need for influence. Such factors could constitute negative correlates of the readiness to change the nature of programme implementation and development functioning and, therefore, of the concern to improve development performance.

These findings bring out the importance, as discussed in Chapter 1, of leadership values in promoting a concern for change in the nature and status of the functioning of our development programmes. Democratic-empowering values are likely to improve the programme implementation in this respect by weakening the tendency for prescriptive problem-solving. The data also showed a somewhat disturbing situation regarding workplace functioning. The 'status quoist' functionaries seemed to enjoy greater creature comforts and, maybe, more influence at the workplace. The critics of the system who desired to improve the implementation and functioning of development were not so rewarded.

Correlates of Low and High Cadre Mentality

Both the factor analysis as well as the multiple regression analysis, as discussed before and in Chapter 5, showed that cadre mentality played a unique role in our administrative functioning. It showed, relatively, a low loading of 0.43 on factor 1 (status quoism in development functioning; see Appendix Table 5.11). It also emerged as the only significant linear predictor of workplace satisfaction (Appendix Tables 5.12 and 6.10). What kind of relationship obtained between this caste like mentality induced and reinforced by the system itself (see Table 5.4 for dimensions of cadre mentality) and other independent variables?

The obtained mean score of 5.17 (Appendix Table 6.4) showed that, on the whole, the agricultural extension scientists and officials tended to agree about the phenomenon of cadre mentality in our administration and development functioning. However, they differed in the strength of their assessment. As low and high, the two groups differed significantly in their mean scores on this tendency (see Appendix Table 6.12). The low group was much more emphatic that the cadre mentality was dysfunctional. Did the strength of such mentality or the members' attachment to some cadre make a difference in their other development behaviours? Data seen in Appendix Tables 6.13 to 6.18 provides some answer.

Some Correlates of Cadre Mentality

The high cadre mentality group showed significantly greater tendency to deny that our administration and development functioning suffered from centralisation. Overall, they were much more status quoist and tended to deny that the development functioning suffered from any dysfunctional tendency. They felt that, on the whole, it was okay. They enjoyed significantly greater influence and, also, amenities at the workplace. More important, however, was that such functionaries, i.e., those with greater cadre mentality, were much more satisfied and integrated at their workplace than those having comparatively lower cadre mentality.

Thus, cadre mentality emerged as a significant intervening variable, on the one hand, in shaping the attitude of status quoism in development functioning and on the other, in workplace satisfaction with regard to influence, amenities and supervisory behaviour. Interestingly, it made no difference in the perceived nature of the job. Its impact was, therefore, seen only on some aspects of work environment and on the context of work. It was associated more prominently with prestige, perks and power of the 'office' and the 'system', and not so much with social worth and the challenge of development jobs. Clearly, such a mentality was motivated by the need for influence and control. Such functionaries were not so much motivated by a concern for challenge, excellence and better quality of life for the common people. We discuss implications of such behaviour further in Chapter 7.

Content of Cadre Mentality

In view of the importance of cadre mentality in the functioning of both the workplace and the development programmes, it would be useful to clearly understand its content and meaning. The three items which measured it, or status quoism, in this respect were as follows:

(1) Civil servants are very particular about their seniority in their cadre and generally try to get posting as per their seniority.
(2) Civil servants are eager to maintain their separate cadre and generally talk about their cadre superiority.
(3) It is often said that civil servants tend to consider their service as better than others and want to maintain its distinctiveness.

These items, more or less, reflect the existing situation in our cadre-based administration and public services. It is well known that such a system prevented inter-departmental linkages and harmonious management of programmes (Mehta, 1989a: 50–52). The items mentioned here, unlike other items in the same instrument, do not refer to development programme. These are neutral without suggesting any positive or negative implications for development performance. On the whole, the functionaries here agreed that such a cadre mentality did exist. There were variations only in the degree of their agreement. Those who agreed less were subjectively different from those who agreed more. Lesser the agreement, greater was the cadre mentality and defence of the present system. Such persons also showed greater support for the present nature of development functioning. They showed much stronger attitude of status quoism in this respect.

The findings showed the importance of cadre mentality in the functioning of a given work organisation. Those showing greater support for the system, i.e., higher cadre mentality, were also more satisfied with their work environment. Such satisfaction made them complacent about the tendency for centralisation, and the nature of programme implementation and development functioning in general. The attitude to the structure of our administration, thus, emerged as an important factor in both the functioning of the workplace as well as development with significant implications for performance.

Variance in Behaviour at a State Enterprise

As mentioned before, the same instruments (see Chapter 5) were applied to managers and workmen at a state mines and minerals enterprise. In several respects, the findings there were similar to those discussed earlier. Thus, dominative leadership was found to be associated more with a low sense of efficacy. In their case, education made a difference in this respect. No or very little education contributed to social backwardness as reflected in the dominative leadership values. Education was also an important positive factor in their leadership value system. More educated members of the organisation tended to show greater preference for motivating-empowering values. Interestingly, education was also an important factor in their sense of efficacy, particularly in the sense of initiative. Lower the level of education, lower was the sense of initiative and lower the sense of initiative, greater was the preference for dominative leadership values. It was interesting that at this enterprise, engaged in processing an important mineral using high technology, education made a significant difference in the use of technology for improving the quality of production.

Education was also an important factor in the members' perception of their influence and participation at the workplace. More educated members were less satisfied in this respect. Generally, they (in this case, mostly the managers) showed a sense of powerlessness. It seemed that the objective conditions at the workplace catered more to the needs of less educated members. It was, therefore, not surprising that during the interviews as well as small group discussions, there was a consensus about the need for paying more attention to the quality of production as against only quantity.

Leadership Values/Styles, Efficacy and Sense of Vigilance

Vigilance is always an essential requirement in mining operations. Here, the leadership values and sense of efficacy were found to be significant factors in members sense of vigilance. Lower the sense of vigilance, greater was the tendency for patronising values. Sense of reflective thinking was also an important factor in this respect. Greater the desire/readiness for seeking challenges and for undertaking innovative behaviour, greater was the sense of vigilance. Theoretically, it was an important finding that members' tendency to reflect on their performance and abilities significantly contributed to raising the sense of vigilance in the organisation. The same was true for the need for social achievement. Greater such a need, greater was the sense of vigilance. It showed that members' collective imagination and concern for overall development performance and production contributed significantly to the overall sense of vigilance in the organisation.

Workplace Satisfaction

Members showing greater concern for excellence at the workplace were less satisfied with their influence and participation in the organisation. Greater the interest of members in achieving quality in performance and improving production and development performance and greater their initiative, lower was their satisfaction with influence and participation as well as welfare available to them in the organisation.

Welfare, Self-esteem and Mental Health

Another very important theoretical finding was that employees' welfare at the workplace and their satisfaction on this account was a significant positive factor in promoting sense of self-esteem. Not only such amenities enhanced production at the workplace, they also promoted self-esteem among the members of the organisation. The findings here tended to confirm the hypothesis about macro-economic policy and withdrawal of the state and other such agencies from welfare programmes, and the weakening of social dimension of work lowering the sense of self-esteem and, thereby, harming the mental health of the employees.[4]

Work Amenities, Reflective Thinking and Job Satisfaction

It was interesting that welfare and amenities available at the workplace along with supervisory behaviour also emerged as a very significant factor in job satisfaction. These findings provided confirmation of the relationship between the context of work and the content of job (Mehta, 1978). Further, sense of reflective thinking and job satisfaction showed a striking relationship. Organisational members who tended to be more reflective, i.e., who were stimulated more by the challenge involved in their work and tended to take an 'actor' role in this respect were also more satisfied with their job. Theoretically, it was an important finding (see Table 5.1) that those not goaded to work, maybe by monetary incentives and/or by coercion, but those stimulated by reasoning and challenge-taking were the creative members of the organisation. They were satisfied more when challenged by the nature and social worth of their work. It also provided support to the relationship between mental health and nature of job at the workplace. It was interesting in this respect that working independently in small groups to discuss various problems and needs of their organisation, the members themselves perceived that quality of work was not necessarily served by an incentive scheme which primarily depended on the quantity of production.[5]

Research Hypotheses and Propositions

These findings regarding development problem-solving and other related behaviours provided confirmation for some important research hypotheses for psychological audit and suggested some leads for HRD and other intervention. These are briefly summarised here and discussed in Chapter 7.

(1) Subordinate-superior relationship at the workplace (as informed by respect for subordinates' ideas, appreciation of their work and positive image of their capability) contributes to the members/functionaries' approach in dealing with the needs and problems of the people. More dissatisfied they are with the supervisory behaviours and practices, greater the tendency in them for dependency inducing behaviour.

(2) Cadre mentality (and the cadre system of administration) contributes to a sense of complacency at the work organisation as well as in development functioning.

(3) Social policies and welfare amenities at the workplace contribute to members' sense of self-esteem.

(4) Acquiescence may be acceptance of the Rentier-Dole practices contributes to dependency inducing problem-solving behaviour in development.

(5) Education among the traditionally disadvantaged people is an important factor in curbing social backwardness and in promoting democratic-empowering values and psychological empowerment in them.

(6) Motivating-empowering leadership behaviour greatly contributes to: sense of vigilance, positive thinking about others' capability and the tendency to promote capability in subordinates and other people.

(7) Sense of reflective thinking contributes to weakening of the dependency inducing problem-solving behaviour.

(8) Sense of reflective thinking contributes to the readiness for undertaking challenge at the workplace and in development programmes.

(9) Dominative-cum-patronising leadership values weaken the sense of initiative in the organisation.

(10)   Dominative-disempowering leadership values greatly contribute
        to dependency inducing behaviour in development functionaries
        as well as at the workplace.

(11)   Capability promoting problem-solving behaviour significantly
        contributes to positive thinking about others' capability which,
        in turn, promotes sense of vigilance in the organisation.

(12)   Sense of vigilance is an important weakener of dominative patron-
        ising leadership behaviour. Greater the sense of vigilance, lower
        is the preference for dominative values.

Notes

1. For details regarding the concept and scoring of these needs, see Mehta (1994c: 198–202) and for the scoring system, see the appendix there.
2. For details and discussion of these findings, see Mehta 1999.
3. The same method was followed in the study of mines and minerals personnel, as discussed later.
4. For discussion of such relationship between macro-economic policy, workplace and human development, see Mehta 1994a.
5. For details regarding small group work and interviews, see the report on the state-run enterprise of mines and minerals, Mehta 1999.

SEVEN

Democratising Work and Development Processes: Socio-psychological Monitoring for Interventions

Social Organisation and Development Functioning

The traditional social organisation has been a source of operation and exploitation, as discussed in Chapter 1, for the vast number of labouring people in the country. Over the years, it has sought to inculcate a negative image of physical labour, along with negative affect for themselves among the labouring classes/castes. The British colonial rule reinforced such an unequal organisation in order to impose its ideology of being a superior class as 'rulers' and the labouring people, as 'subjects' and the 'ruled'. They capitalised on the prevailing social conditions and beliefs and behaved as 'landlords' and 'headmasters'. It was interesting to note that they promoted Dharmashastras almost as civic code thus cementing a mutually beneficial relationship with the brahminical order.

These powerful historical antecedents have continued reinforcing political processes, policies and administrative tendencies even after independence. The state, therefore, got more and more distanced from the common people. Besides biased policies, development functioning has been marked by tendencies such as dominative leadership styles and exclusionary communication, contributing to its poor performance in terms of even the basic needs of the people.

In spite of the poor development performance and the negative behaviour of the state, there has been a tremendous expansion of democratic and egalitarian aspirations among the common people. They are now no longer willing to accept the age-old authority structure. The traditional social order is being confronted by a new power system being generated by the electoral democratic processes. At the same time, the neo-liberal economic policies are set to give primacy to the market forces and reduce the role of the state in development. The 'have nots', as the experience shows (Chapter 1), tend to be at the suffering end of such neo-liberal policies. As the President recently remarked,

> One half of our society guzzles aerated beverages while the other has to make do with palmfuls of muddied water. Our three-way fast lane of liberalization, privatisation and globalisation must provide safe pedestrian crossings for the unempowered India also so that it too can move towards 'Equality of Status and Opportunity'.[1]

The role of the state in promoting social and human development and egalitarian economic development thus continues to be very much on the agenda.

People's Movements: Asking for Better Performance

Dalit and similar other people's movements have contributed to the emerging socio-political changes in the country. The deprived people tend not only to vote more than the traditionally-entrenched elites but also to show greater interest in the democratic institutions. They desire to establish political linkages and to approach their daily needs and problems via political mobilisation. They now tend to question the performance of various governments (Chapter 1). There are clear signals of a growing feeling that the elected representatives did not care and pay attention to their needs and problems; that the relationship between the people and the government officials was not cordial; and that the attitude of the police towards people was not humane. Such critical evaluation is a distinct departure from the past which indicates the growing democratisation in society and adds further meaning to the enhanced sense of political and social efficacy among the people. No wonder, therefore, that the same people who voted the government with a huge mandate are now seen to turn against it.

Promises and Practice

The role of the state (and the state and other development functionaries) has to be, therefore, viewed and evaluated in the context of such emerging aspirations for better development performance. For example, it is pertinent to ask in this respect: in whose interest, rules and regulations are approached? Even in the context of the neo-liberal economic policy (which repeatedly pleads for the need for competition), it is necessary to enhance competitiveness at various levels, particularly among the deprived and marginalised people. The important message of last some electoral verdicts, as mentioned earlier, is the felt need of the people for improving their skills, their income and the quality of their life. If democracy has to have any meaning, it has to address such concerns. In other words, there has to be more and more democratisation in order to improve both governance and development performance. This calls for reconceptualisation of development and serious thinking about the values, attitudes and behaviours of the development functionaries.

There has been a continuous gap between the promises and the actual development practice in the country. Though the Constitution of India guarantees equity of status and opportunity, it is now necessary to ask: status in what? opportunities for what? As the President recently noted,

> Fifty years into our life in the Republic we find that Justice—social, economic and political—remains an unrealised dream for millions of our fellow citizens. The benefits of our economic growth are yet to reach them. We have one of the world's largest reservoirs of technical personnel but also the world's largest number of illiterates; the world's largest middle class but also the largest number of people below the poverty line and the largest number of children suffering from mal-nutrition.[2]

In such a situation, if we pay just lip-service to the constitution and treat all people equally, we may land up reinforcing the age-old inequality. Non-fulfilment of basic needs of the deprived not only perpetuates mass destitution but also tends to reinforce the unequal social organisation and fuel caste feelings and communal attitudes. It is, therefore, imperative for the state to perform certain duties so that weaker people can exercise their rights without the strong and privileged always prevailing over them.

The United Nations have declared that the people have a right to development. It also specifies that development practice has to be informed by transparency, accountability, participation of people and equity of access. This right, however, remains to be fulfilled for millions of our people. How long should 'unempowered India' continue to wait for the equality of status and opportunity? As the President cautioned the country, 'beware of the fury of the patient long suffering people'.[3]

Moving from Promises to Practice

There is, thus, a growing urgency for moving from promises to practice, and for providing more democratic governance and basic needs of the people at the ground level. As the President recently said, 'Why is it that as a nation we do not feel the desperate urgency of making our people literate? I hope that vested interests have not been fearful of awakening the masses through education. On the contrary, we should have faith in the people. We should organise a mass movement for literacy.'[4]

There is an urgent need for improving development practice, not only for effective implementation of the constitutional directives but also for carrying out much needed structural changes, and for helping people participate in movements and in governance. There is, thus, a need for democratising governance and the development process. This would mean changing the entrenched power-equation, where liberal democracy is more concerned with people rather than with things, in order to help them to not only survive but also move ahead with hope and confidence.

Empowering the Civil Society

People's movements, NGDOs and the civil society in general have an important role to play in democratising governance and the development processes. They have an adversarial role to play in curtailing the increasing insensitivity and authoritarianism of the state, and in confronting traditional social order (see Chapter 1). At the same time, the civil society can work as a link between the individual and the state for promoting and protecting the rights and freedom of all citizens irrespective of religion, caste, community or gender, particularly those of the minorities and the socio-economically weaker sections of society. Thus, open, secular and democratic institutions of civil society can greatly contribute to replacing the political and social order based on inborn hierarchy, by a system based on equal rights of individuals. In fact, this is the defining feature of democracy as well as development, i.e., to address the basic needs and rights of all individuals. It is important to ensure that disadvantaged people have equal access to assets that are valued in society. Without such access, equal rights guaranteed by the Indian Constitution cannot be achieved.

The civil society itself, however, needs to be mobilised and activated for such democratisation and for achieving the various developmental goals. For example, there are institutions which could be efficient but insensitive to the need of equal rights for all. Development functionaries, including those placed in the civil society such as in NGDOs, need to show such sensitivity and perceive such goals energetically. Similarly, corporations need to function in a way that promotes the welfare of all, protect the interest of the society and encourage development of capacities that enable individuals to become active members of the civil society. This, in turn, would help put pressure and raise demand on the state to carry out its various constitutional and development obligations.[5]

Objective and Subjective Factors in Work and Development

Objective Conditions of Work and Concern for Excellence

Research reported in previous chapters suggests some pointers which could help in understanding the development processes and in evaluating and monitoring performance at the workplace, civil society and in development programmes. For example, with other factors controlled, there was a clear relationship between work satisfaction and concern for excellence at the workplace. It showed the importance of objective conditions of work as represented by influence, participation and welfare amenities available at the workplace and the nature of job and supervisory practices. The nature of the entrenched social structure conditions the dominant elite to be interested much more in power and in maintaining the status quo in this respect rather than achievement and excellence in their field of work. It was interesting that such need for influence was associated more with disempowering and authoritarian values. This is, in a sense, a paradoxical situation that the functionaries, whether in government organisations, or elsewhere who are responsible for development show less concern for good performance and more concern for dominative power. As we know, a concern for seeking excellence in development could be an important resource for improving the on-going programmes in the country. As the President reminded the nation, 'One reason why our infrastructure remains weak is that the quality of civil work executed is poor—compromised by sub-standard materials, corrupt practices and sloppy supervision. We ignore the social dimension of our actions and practices'.[6]

Interest and concern for good performance is a crucial factor for achieving the stated goals of development, i.e., for promoting capability in people and improving their quality of life. However, the traditional craving for status and power works as a very significant weakener of such an achievement concern (Chapter 6). As the President reminded us, 'far too many of us lack the professional pride to see a task well performed, a responsibility well borne'.[7] As the present research (Chapter 5) has shown, such a concern—for 'task well performed', for 'responsibility well borne', for better development performance, for more accountable governance—is significantly correlated with the nature and structure of workplace functioning. The objective and subjective conditions of work are, thus, highly and intimately interrelated. This is particularly true for a sense of pride in social worthiness and for quality in development performance.

Sense of Vigilance, Workplace and Development Functioning

Lack of or low vigilance seems to be an endemic phenomenon in the country. No search is required for evidence as this can be observed almost everywhere—in simple to difficult situations.[8] Thus, the need to enhance vigilance in the country, whether at the workplace or in various development situations, can hardly be over-emphasised. Interestingly, managers and workmen who favoured motivating-empowering leadership values also showed significantly greater sense of vigilance. Lower the tendency for democratic-empowering values, lower is the sense of vigilance. In other words, greater the inclination for dominative values, lower is the level of vigilance in the organisation. It was interesting to find those given to patronising, sermonising and lecturing to subordinates themselves showing significantly a lower sense of vigilance. Vigilance is an essential requirement in production situations like mining operations. Its importance in matters of national security and elsewhere can hardly be over-emphasised. It was, therefore, interesting that value system and a sense of pride in excellence were also important correlates of the sense of vigilance, as of good governance and development performance.

The sense of reflective thinking was another important factor in sense of vigilance and in the members' perception of others' capability at the workplace. It is necessary for any creative and democratic society to value capability of its people. Reflective thinking—readiness to ponder over development needs and problems and to undertake challenge in this respect—as our research showed, greatly helped in appreciating other persons' worth and, thus, in strengthening capabilities in society. The organisation leaders who were positive about the worth of their subordinates and peers showed not only a greater sense of vigilance but also greater readiness for developing their capability at the workplace. Inculcation and release of such sensitivity, therefore, could be an important resource for improving the level of vigilance, care and production at the workplace as well as the quality of performance in development programmes.[9] That is why, generation of capacity for reflective thinking is by itself an important goal of development.[10]

Reflective thinking is particularly important in our context, where functionaries—whether in development or even at an industrial enterprise—are prone to give greater importance to targets and numbers (i.e., quantity) and to showing just token interest in the desired performance.[11] Strengthening of the readiness for seeking challenge and of reflective thinking could help in motivating the functionaries to achieve quality and the social goals of development. Similarly, the release of sense of reflective thinking and efficacy in the people themselves, via mobilisation, organisation and training, could help generate the 'demand' for good governance and better performance in government and other programmes.

Dominative Leadership Values and Sense of Personal Efficacy

Dominative leadership values were found to be accompanied by a low sense of personal efficacy. It was an important theoretical finding, which showed that members given to bossing and dominating over people were really low in the sense of power. The dominative leadership was more a symptom of their sense of insecurity and powerlessness. It was interesting that such dominative members in the organisation also showed a low sense of vigilance. They tended to replicate similar behaviour by inducing and reinforcing dependency in their subordinates, and the people in general. They also thought low of their peers', subordinates' and others' capability. On the other hand, efficacious functionaries, as mentioned before, were more likely to promote capability in people. The motivating-empowering leadership values contributed to capability promoting development behaviour and empowerment of the concerned people. Such a value system was, thus, a very important resource for good governance and development performance.

Education and Concern for Collective Excellence

Education (of workers) emerged as a significant factor in the concern for collective excellence and quality at the workplace and also, in their sense of efficacy. As mentioned earlier, greater the sense of efficacy, particularly the sense of reflective thinking, greater was the vigilance in the organisation. And, greater the level of education (particularly among the workforce), greater was the reflective thinking as well as the concern for excellence at the workplace. Human development, particularly literacy and elementary education, is, therefore, one of the most practical social requirements for helping people to think in terms of quality of life, excellence in their work, vigilance in various activities and being more positive about their peers and others in the organisation. Even a small shift in the level of education—from no education to some education, i.e., literacy—produced significant increase in their sense of efficacy (Mehta, 1981). This was amply confirmed by the findings obtained from managers and workmen (see Chapter 6). This also showed the importance of civil society's participation in competitive electoral politics, in people's movements and in development processes. Such participation is a great source of 'non-formal' education and of strengthening people's self-esteem and efficacy (Mehta, 1983, 1994a).

Workplace and Development

The findings, as briefly discussed earlier, highlight the importance of leadership at the programme implementation level, whether political, bureaucratic or non-governmental on the one hand, and of active people's participation in development, on the other. The traditional social orientation of the elite functionaries and their exclusiveness tended to retard development performance. However, sensitivity to people's welfare, egalitarian and empowering values, and the concern for obtaining social goals could work as great human resources for democratisation and development in the country. In this respect, as briefly mentioned before, our research showed the significance of the interface of work organisation and development, and the importance of the functioning of both in shaping social attitudes and behavioural responses of the functionaries.

Social Climate: Home, School and Workplace Environments

The home and school environments are well-known factors in the development of children's attitudes and values. This was confirmed rather strongly by the present research. Fathers' educational level was an important factor in the children's socio-political attitudes. Children of more educated fathers were significantly less conservative and authoritarian in their attitudes/values than those whose fathers had low education. Even some education made a difference in their children's attitudes in this respect (see Figure 4.1). The same was true of social prejudice (towards other social groups). Children of fathers with low or some education showed significantly greater social prejudice than those whose fathers had more education (see Figure 4.2). On the other hand, children studying in government-managed schools were less conservative and authoritarian than those studying in some 'parochially'-managed private school (see Figure 4.3). The same was true of social prejudice and secular mentality. Children in government-managed schools showed not only less social prejudice but also greater tendency for secular attitudes as compared to those studying in parochially managed 'Hindu' or 'Muslim' school (see Figure 4.4).

The interaction of home environment, as indicated by fathers' educational level, and the school environment, as indicated by the nature of school management, showed a very significant impact on children's attitudes and values. Those living and growing up in parochial home-cum-parochial school environment (PPE) were definitely less secular in their attitudes as compared to those being brought up under secular home-cum-secular school environment (SSE) (see Figure 4.5). Similarly, children being brought up under parochial environments were definitely more socially prejudiced as compared to those living and studying under secular environments (see Figure 4.6).

As noted in Chapter 1, there are parallel movements going on in the civil society of the country. On the one hand, there is a growing movement for democratising society for more equitable development and for better performance. On the other hand, there are enhanced efforts to derail this process by dividing the people along communal and religious lines. For example, education, which could become a powerful force for liberating people from the age-old social backwardness and obscurantist practices, is being subverted and 'managed' to spread communal and authoritarian mentality in children. There are attempts to parochialise academic institutions, and rewrite textbooks and change the liberal character of education guaranteed in the constitution.[12] With the increasing democratic upsurge for reversing the power paradigm, the protagonists of the traditional social order also tend to use various techniques to manipulate and thwart the constitution and the onward movement for a more egalitarian society. The school and the home, thus, play a very significant role in socialising children towards secular, liberal and democratic attitudes. However, as the things stand today, and as the number of privately-managed schools increases, the parochially-oriented environment there (and/or at home) could, on the contrary, significantly weaken the movement for democratisation.[13]

The work environment either at a workplace or in a development programme, i.e., the social climate, as the present research showed, was also an important factor in shaping and/or reinforcing dominative or liberal, democratic and empowering leadership values. Such values, in turn, were very important in inculcating the much-needed capability promoting problem-solving development behaviour in the concerned functionaries. These were also important correlates of the readiness to learn and to effect mid-course corrections for improving the quality of development performance. Social climate, whether at home, school, workplace or the field level where the programme has to be implemented, therefore, was a crucial factor in attaining the desired goals of development.

Thus, both the objective as well as subjective conditions, whether at the workplace, the school or at the field of development, were important for achieving social and economic goals towards greater democratisation of society and the polity of the country. As seen in the next section, there is a big and widening gap between the constitutional directives and the obligations put on the state on the one hand, and the actual achievements and the situation obtaining for the people on the ground, on the other.

The Constitution and Its Implementation

The Constitution of India in its Preamble guarantees justice—social, economic and political, liberty of thought, expression, belief, faith and worship, equality of status and fraternity, assuring the dignity of the individual. It provides several fundamental rights including equality before law, abolition of untouchability and prohibition of discrimination on grounds of religion, race, caste, sex and place of birth. The directive principles direct the state, among other things, to secure for the citizens: adequate means of livelihood, right to work, education and public assistance: just and humane conditions of work; living wages, etc.; participation of workers in management of industries; free and compulsory education up to 14 years of age (the state was directed to fulfil this task by 25 January 1960, i.e., 10 years after the promulgation of the constitution). It directs the state to promote the educational and economic interests of SCs/STs and protect them from social injustice and exploitation, and to raise the level of nutrition and standard of living, and to improve public health.

The Preamble, the Fundamental Rights and the Directive Principles of the State Policy together form the conscience of the constitution. It imposes both legal and moral obligations on the state (and the various functionaries) to provide just and reasonable quality of life to all people and to take affirmative action in favour of the weaker sections in all spheres of life. The reality, however, is that even after more than 50 years of the constitution, the state, as represented by the central and the various state governments, has failed to fulfil its obligations to the people. As a result, millions of people are forced to live under sub-human conditions.

The Performance on the Ground

Contrary to the constitutional obligations, there is a growing feeling in the disadvantaged sections of society that the governments hardly protect the interests of the poor for whom the development programmes are, in the first place, publicised. People are increasingly realising that the interest of the powerful prevails over the interest of the weak. Repeated electoral verdicts, as discussed before, show this increasing articulation on the part of the weaker sections. The growing need for implementing promises to the people also underlines the importance of people's movements and mobilisation of the civil society so that the state can be prevailed upon to honour the constitutional directives. Activisation of the civil society, particularly the organisation of the excluded sections of society, could greatly contribute to achieving greater democratisation and the various development goals. Poor development performance underlies the importance not only of appropriate policy making but also, and more importantly, proper implementation of development programmes and policies on the ground.

In the ultimate analysis, the success of any development programme has to be judged in terms of its goals and objectives and concrete perform-ance on the ground, i.e., its impact towards improving the quality of life of the people in general. However, such development performance is intimately impacted by the values, attitudes and behaviour of the develop-ment functionaries. The continuing mass illiteracy, poverty, malnutrition, infant and maternal mortality, public health and sanitation conditions and now, the grim water situation (i.e., in the year 2000) in various parts of the country, succinctly define the on-going development practices and behaviour. It has been estimated that the water table has dipped below 500 metres, in no less than 15 per cent of the land mass, another 27 per cent is on the verge of desertification and large tracts in several states of the country are in perennial grip of drought. Millions of people in states like Rajasthan, Gujarat, some parts of Maharashtra, Madhya Pradesh, Andhra Pradesh, Jammu and Kashmir, Himachal Pradesh, Orissa, West Bengal and Tamil Nadu have been forced to struggle just to get some water.[14]

Such a serious drought has, however, not appeared suddenly. There is a long history of water scarcity and famines in the country, affecting mil-lions of people year after year. What is unique about the drought in this new millennium is that it is the worst ever in the past 100 years. The ravages of extreme water shortage have spread like an epidemic through these various states. The magnitude of the calamity is shown by the tragic fact that Rajasamand Lake (in Udaipur, Rajasthan) built in 1660 to tide over scarcity of water and famine, and which has served the needs of the local people for these centuries has, for the first time, completely dried up. It is the same story everywhere in rural Rajasthan where all rivers, wells, traditional 'haudas' for storing water, streams and rivulets have gone dry.[15]

Such a drought situation is largely man-made which dramatically shows the utter failure of the government to plan for and address the basic needs of the people. It shows that the state machinery comes to some activity only when there is an extreme emergency like a drought situation. Year after year, their reaction mostly has been to sink more tube-wells which, in fact, further aggravates the reasons for drought by depleting the water resources and further lowering the water table.

Another significant dimension of this unfolding tragedy is that there has been a long history and the time-tested wisdom of the people for water harvesting and management in, precisely, the states where drought is taking a heavy toll such as Rajasthan and Gujarat. The state government functionaries, instead of utilising and learning from such experience and wisdom, tend to exclude the people from planning, policy making and implementation. Thus, not only are the people's skills and experience not appreciated and utilised, the state functionaries tend to create a sense of despondency and dependency. The people are forced to unlearn their valuable skills. However, the people's energy cannot be all-together erased by governments' apathy and negative approach. There are stories of people's initiative in the extremely difficult situation of a drought-prone area. Hirve Bazar, a small village in Ahmednagar district of Maharashtra provides one shining example of self-help and people's capability in this respect. The area gets about 450 mm of rainfall annually. By proper harvesting and management of this water, the people have not only been able to preserve it but also to use it efficiently for growing foodgrains and acquire self-sufficiency in this matter. The secret of their prosperity lies in their ability to use and harvest water judicially. People like these villagers help recharge wells and not mindlessly exploit the available water. Increasing documentation of the water problem shows the traditional skills and concerns of the people for water harvesting and for obtaining other infrastructure for themselves. Recently, the President, Shri K.R. Narayanan took an unconventional step to travel to Alwar (Rajasthan) to honour a NGDO and the people for their unique accomplishment of greening the area and even reviving a dead river. Similar success stories are available from some other areas of the country as well which demonstrate the efficacy of local water harvesting efforts and extraordinary degree of local initiative, participation and motivation in developmental efforts. Such participatory development in critical sectors like water management brings out not only the apathy of the state functionaries but also provides a sad commentary on them, that people were able to achieve such success because the government was absent from the scene. [16] The officials are given to chase targets and not to involve farmers and people in such important matters of life and death for them. The officials register societies but leave out people's participation though it is they who have the skills and who understand how to deal with land and water. On the contrary, the engineers and officials who intervene, only sap people's initiative and their ability. Ironically, success in villages like Hirve Bazar has come because 'the government is absent there'. [17]

Functioning of the Constitution: Criteria for Evaluating Performance

Although the Constitution of India calls for a 'socialist' and a 'welfare-oriented' state, in practice, it has really got separated and away from the people. The dismal development performance should persuade us to consider, as the President recently remarked, 'whether it is the Constitution that has failed us or whether it is we who have failed the Constitution'.[18] The constitution lays down several criteria which could help us to evaluate development performance and the behaviour of the government as well as the non-government development functionaries in this respect. For example, the constitution clearly requires the state, i.e., the central and various state governments to protect the interest of the weaker sections and promote egalitarian social and economic development. However, we have not been able to fulfil, not only the promises made from time to time to the people but even the constitutional directives in this respect. The actual development performance not only has been lagging much behind the promises but many a times the impact of such efforts has been contrary to the welfare of the people. The continuing poor quality of life, for at least half the population, is a standing judgement on the performance of the government(s). Besides the policies, the values, attitudes and behaviour of the various functionaries, as briefly summarised in the section on Objective and Subjective Factors, are also important causes of such poor performance. It would, therefore, be useful to study the various facets of such attitudes and behaviours so that the programmes can be properly monitored and also, a mechanism instituted for mid-course corrections and better achievements. Some such criteria to evaluate the functioning of development can be stated as follows:

Criteria for Evaluating Development Functioning

(1) To find out to what extent the development functionaries are democratic, secular and egalitarian in their values. These constitute important intervening variables which could throw light on whether or not they work in the interest of the disadvantaged and deprived people for whom the programmes are particularly meant in the first place.

(2) Do development functionaries address the needs and aspirations of people who now increasingly articulate the desire for a better

quality of life? How much sensitivity do they show to such needs and problems of the people? It would be pertinent in this respect to find out, to what extent do they help the deprived people in acquiring capability and initiative for solving their own problems? Or do they behave to reinforce and induce dependency in them. Examples of success stories as mentioned earlier, show that it is the initiative of the people which makes all the difference in the actual performance on the ground. It is, therefore, necessary to understand whether the functionaries help release such initiative and capability or cripple these.

(3) As there is now a growing urgency for bridging the gap between promises and actual practice, and as governance is required to address the basic needs of the people, it is necessary to understand the fears and hopes of the development functionaries themselves. For example, do they have faith in the people? Or are they afraid of promoting capability and awakening in the masses?

(4) The traditional social organisation promotes a strong craving for power and domination in the functionaries and other elite. Such motivation drives them to maintain the status quo and to show only a token interest in development programmes. On the contrary, pride in social achievement and accomplishments in terms of social goals of development is very important for success in development efforts. It is, therefore, necessary to understand the strength of their needs for power and domination and for achievement and excellence. Such concerns can make all the difference in the quality of performance on the ground and in accelerating the process of democratising development and governance in the country. It is, therefore, necessary not only to evaluate development in terms of such concerns of the functionaries but also to monitor programmes on the ground along these lines. If the functionaries continue to ignore the social dimension of their action and practice, then the development performance on the ground is bound to be sloppy and poor.

(5) The system of work and the objective conditions prevailing at the workplace play a significant role in shaping subjective conditions, as reflected in the attitudes, values and behaviour of the functionaries at the workplace. It is, therefore, necessary to have a continual audit of the workplace. For example, how far is the

workplace/work organisation/development organisation sensitive to promoting participation of the members and how far do work policies cater to the welfare of the employees? Such objective conditions and work-related policies have a direct bearing on the values, efficacy, self-esteem and initiative of the employees. These, in turn, significantly impact their behaviour on the ground and, thus, the quality of development performance. Thus, there is a need for specifically designed studies of such relevant object-ive conditions of work and policy at the workplace. It is necessary to institute continuous monitoring of such policies and factors in order to be able to institute mid-course corrections for improving the on-going development performance.

(6) Sense of vigilance is another very crucial factor for obtaining the desired quality in governance as well as in development performance. Sense of vigilance needs to be monitored on a continuous basis whether at the workplace or in development programme or in other situations of governance and elsewhere in the country. The values, attitudes and motivation of the func-tionaries have a significant impact on their sense of vigilance. It is, therefore, necessary to have an audit of the various aspects of vigilance behaviour as well as the conditions which promote or demote vigilance in various fields of activities. As the value system and sense of pride in excellence are important correlates of the sense of vigilance, it is necessary to understand these so that vigilance can be properly monitored and improved.

(7) Sense of reflective thinking is another important and crucial factor in, not only, the sense of vigilance but also, for obtaining capabil-ity for better development performance. Readiness to ponder and analyse the various causes and aspects of development per-formance could greatly help both the development functionaries and the people to undertake challenges in this respect. Sense of reflective thinking, therefore, is by itself an important goal of development. How strong is this tendency in the functionaries and how ready are they to help develop it in the people? Such questions become all the more important in our situation where the functionaries are given to pay greater attention to targets and numbers, and procedures and formalities rather than to the goals of development. It is, therefore, necessary to evaluate the

various factors relating to reflective thinking and also, to monitor programmes in this regard.

(8) Empowerment of people is another important goal of development. The traditional dominative leadership and dependency inducing tendency in the functionaries and elsewhere are significant inhibiting intervening variables in this respect. Such 'dominative' functionaries are also known to be low in their own sense of personal efficacy. They tend to replicate similer powerlessness and dependency in people on the ground. It is, therefore, necessary to institute studies to understand and monitor various aspects relating to sense of personal efficacy of both the functionaries and the people.

(9) Social mobilisation, organisation and collective assertion on the part of the people help in promoting and releasing reflective thinking in them. Mass movements also need to be evaluated on this basis: to what extent these strengthen reflective thinking and release initiative in the civil society, and to what extent such movements help achieve the desired goals of development on the ground.

(10) Education is a crucial factor for promoting better quality of life in the country. It is important for empowerment and capability in the deprived and disadvantaged people. The functionaries' attitude to education such as literacy and primary education, can make a difference in this respect. It is necessary to find out how interested they are in promoting these crucial social inputs. Similarly, people's movements and social mobilisation also need to be evaluated on this count. How far do such movements promote education and awareness among the people. It is necessary to monitor both the functioning of governance and the various people's movements in civil society in this respect.

(11) Social environment is crucial whether at home, in school, at the workplace or at a development programme on the ground. Such an environment evolves as a result of the interaction of the functionaries vis-a-vis the people. Monitoring of the social environment in development functioning or in the functioning of school and workplace is, therefore, important for obtaining the constitutional directives and the social goals of development. Does

such an environment promote authoritarian and dogmatic attitudes in children and/or in people? Or does it promote and strengthen democratic and egalitarian values and attitudes? It is necessary in this respect, to study the various aspects of such social environment and to monitor the values, attitudes and behaviours of the concerned functionaries to ensure progress towards democratisation of work and development processes in the country.

Democratising Work and Development Processes: Evaluation, Monitoring and Interventions: Some Propositions

The present research studies, thus, provided confirmation of some important research hypotheses (summarised in Chapter 6) and suggested some new ones. These could form the bases of criteria for designing evaluation and monitoring of programme functioning and interventions for democratising the development processes for achieving the desired goals of socio-economic progress. Some such propositions and suggested interventions can be briefly stated as follows:

Propositions:

(1) Dominative Leadership Reinforces Dependency in People.

Traditionally-oriented development functionaries with dominative leadership are likely to reinforce dependency behaviour in the common people. Weakening of such values and strengthening of democratic and egalitarian leadership could help promote initiative, efficacy and capability in people and, in turn, enhance democratisation in the civil society.

(2) Concern for Performance and Achievement Moderates the Traditional Craving for Status and Power.

The entrenched craving for status and influence among the elite is accompanied by dominative leadership values. Such a need for authoritarian influence could be weakened/moderated by strengthening the concern for achievement and performance. This would help in strengthening the democratic and empowering leadership values and, in turn, in improving the functioning of development programmes.

(3) Realisation that Programmes are Means to Obtain Welfare of the People Improves Development Functioning.

The need for achievement in the functionaries could enhance the realisation in them that development programmes are a means to obtain welfare of the people. This, in turn, could help in heightening sensitivity to their needs and problems, and to strengthen openness and readiness to critically assess the functioning of development, and improve performance.

(4) Interface Between and Among Work, Democracy and Development.

Appropriate restructuring and democratisation at the workplace would help strengthen both democracy and development:

(a) the functioning and conditions of work organisation contribute to the functionaries' initiative and sense of efficacy;

(b) the social policies, such as for employee welfare, greatly contribute to their sense of self-esteem;

(c) democratic and empowering behaviour on the part of senior functionaries at the workplace vis-a-vis their subordinates could help release similar leadership values among the latter vis-a-vis the people on the ground;

(d) the functionaries' readiness to critically assess development functioning could be enhanced by infusing a sense of purpose, a sense of pride, challenge and social worth at the workplace. This, in turn, could help in obtaining the stated social goals of development.

Socio-psychological Monitoring and Suggested Interventions: Some Guidelines

The research hypotheses and propositions, as briefly summarised earlier thus, inform some important criteria (section on the Constitution) for predicting development and work-related behaviour and for evaluating programme functioning and monitoring progress in this respect. Such criteria provide some guidelines for planning and designing interventions at several levels such as the civil society, public administration, the workplace and implementation levels. Our research suggests the need for paying attention to three broad sets of interactive variables for interventions designed to energising the development processes (as summarised in Table 7.1).

Table 7.1
Variables in Work and Development Processes:
Some Guidelines for Interventions

Variables			Development Goals
System of Administration	*Workplace Functioning*	*Behavioural*	
Colonial hangover; impact of the traditional caste-based social organisation	Superior-subordinate relationship and supervisory practices	Sense of personal efficacy including initiative, self-esteem and reflective thinking	Effective and adequate fulfilment of basic needs of people
Rentier-Dole practices	Reward policies	Leadership values	Help develop capability, empowerment and organisation
Cadre system	Social planning: welfare, education, skill upgradation	The need for influence and the need for personal and social achievement	Sense of vigilance
Status and exclusion characterised by dominative values	Influence and participation Challenge and social worth of work	Responsiveness and sensitivity to people's problems and needs	

Macro-economic Policy and System of Administration

First and foremost, there was a need to relook at the neo-liberal economic policies and the system of administration. Systemic factors which needed particular attention included variables relating to the nature of social organisation and the functioning of public administration. The traditional unequal social organisation continues to have an impact on the mindset of public functionaries, particularly at the ground level, in development programmes. This is further compounded by the colonial hangover in administration which gives greater importance to cadre, status, exclusion and power rather than achievement and social goals. Our system of administration is also very widely marked by Rentier-Dole practices which inevitably induce dependency in people and curtail their freedom and other rights as equal citizens. The system, therefore, strongly reinforces dominative and exclusionary values in the functionaries.

The neo-liberal economic policies which seek to weaken the state role in development (Mehta, 1994a) were likely to reinforce dominative leadership values in public officials on the one hand, and induce dependency in people, on the other. Such policies are also likely to reinforce and promote a sense of powerlessness among the affected people (for example, because of downsizing, retrenchment and subsequent unemployment) and injure their efficacy and sense of self-esteem. Such sense of powerlessness is likely to further boost dominative leadership values and dependency inducing tendency in development and managerial behaviour.

Economic policies of liberalisation, privatisation and globalisation (in short, LPG) also tend to change the nature of employer and the concept of work itself. Even the nature of a public sector employer is being shifted from being a model social employer to a model profit earner. This was likely to heighten the sense of insecurity, injure mental health and hinder the inculcation of much-needed capability and competitiveness, thus, impeding both social as well as economic development (Mehta, 2000). As the sense of efficacy and self-esteem were important correlates of motivating empowering leadership values and as both these were significant factors in development behaviour, the unregulated neo-liberal economic policies (LPG) are likely to hamper the process of capacity building, whether at the workplace or in development.

There was a need for taking a relook at such economic policies also, because these are likely to afflict our public administration and, therefore, the development programmes. Widespread public corruption is being further fuelled by high intensity consumerism which is the mainstay of the new policies. This scourge thrives by manipulating people and by inducing a sense of insecurity and dependency in them. The desired development performance is, therefore, not possible without eradicating it.[19] Reforming administration is not so easy also, because of the presence of caste-like distinct 'services' and cadres. The concerned personnel tend to show a kind of in-group feeling and a sense of belonging to their respective cadre. Such 'cadre mentality' was a highly significant factor in workplace complacency. Greater the cadre mentality, greater was the sense of complacency. This (self-satisfaction), in turn, worked as a reciprocal reinforcer of status quoism. Such personnel, therefore, gave strong internal support for continuation of the existing rigid (and corrupt) system of administration. They were likely to resist and defeat efforts for giving a developmental orientation to public administration.[20] Unregulated LPG was also likely to reinforce traditional authoritarian values in our elite, thereby, further widening the gap between them and the large masses of our working people. Such policies provide them with an ideological justification and an alibi for neglecting the social goals of development. Dilution of social purpose is one of the main reasons why such policies end up obtaining just the opposite of what these claim to—weakening of competition, competitiveness, innovativeness and flexibility. Strong interventions are, thus, needed in civil society to pressure the state for humanising and democratising such policies.

It is pertinent here to recall the role which the people—the disadvantaged civil society—can play in this respect. Mass movements and competitive electoral politics, for example (see Chapter 1), tend to generate pressure on the state for more democratic and responsive governance, and for better development performance in terms of their basic needs. Thus, the people have the potential for raising powerful demand on the system, both social and administrative, for greater democratisation in society as well as in development. This suggests the need for greater people mobilisation in civil society via education, organisation and movements. Such efforts could also create the desired socio-political environment for restructuring and reorienting the administration.

Workforce and Functionaries' Behaviour

Systemic variables, as briefly discussed before, have a powerful impact on the objective conditions available at the workplace, and the latter tend to have a significant impact on the functionaries' behaviour (Table 7.1). For instance, the superior-subordinate relationship, supervisory practices, reward policies, nature of social planning, availability of welfare, education and skill upgradation, availability of influence and participation at the workplace, and challenge and social worth of work have a significant impact on the various subjective conditions of the members and the development functionaries. Such objective conditions are very important for inculcating a sense of personal efficacy including initiative, self-esteem and reflective thinking, and in shaping leadership values and individual needs, including the need for personal and social achievement. The functionaries' sense of vigilance as well as their social responsiveness to the needs and problems of the people are also profoundly influenced by the objective conditions of work prevailing at the workplace.

The interaction of the objective conditions of work and the subjective conditions represented in the behavioural variables, in turn, significantly influence the functionaries' development behaviour on the ground. As mentioned earlier, social policy, the availability of welfare at the workplace and other such objective conditions could work as an important factor in the inculcation of self-esteem among the members. Such social policy interventions can, thus, greatly help in weakening dominative values and in enhancing motivating and empowering values among the functionaries. Herein lies the importance of a socially-conscious employer who could play a significant role in strengthening democratisation. Similarly, another policy intervention, i.e., education for example, as found in the mines and minerals enterprise (see Chapter 6), can be an important factor in strengthening democratic leadership values and sense of efficacy and initiative. It is also likely to boost the workers' need for personal achievement and concern for excellence and quality. Even a small upward movement in this respect—from no education to some primary education—has the potential for accelerating human development and democratisation in the country where nearly half the population is still illiterate or almost illiterate. It would, therefore, be very useful to institute studies for continual evaluation of the objective and subjective conditions obtaining at the workplace.

It also shows the need, on the one hand, for policy and structural interventions for providing appropriate conditions of work at the workplace and, on the other, for specifically designed behaviour training interventions. For instance, training designed to boost the need for personal excellence, sense of personal efficacy and democratic leadership values can make a significant contribution to enhancing the functionaries' readiness for promoting capability in people while dealing with their needs and problems. Similarly, an enhanced sense of reflective thinking and the readiness to seek and take challenge in work and development would help weaken the traditional dependency inducing problem-solving behaviour.

Sense of vigilance is obviously an important factor in proper functioning at the workplace as well as in development. Concern for excellence and quality along with a readiness for reflective thinking could greatly contribute to boosting vigilance. Policy interventions for providing ground-level work experience at an enterprise as well as in the context of development could also help in this respect. Such work experience is not ordinarily available to functionaries at the higher levels of work hierarchy. Thus, the experience of working with people on the ground, along with human development designed to boost the need for achievement, reflective thinking and democratic leadership values could enhance the level of vigilance in society as well as at the workplace.

This symbiosis between the objective and subjective conditions underlines the importance of social dimension at the workplace, whether in government or in non-government and other organisations. Such policies were important for strengthening and maintaining self-esteem of the functionaries. These also, very significantly, impact leadership values prevailing in the organisation. Greater the feeling of well-being and being wanted among the members, greater was their concern for quality in development and other performance. The leadership values and related sense of personal efficacy and motivation, therefore, strongly intervened between the objective conditions of work and the functionaries' development behaviour on the ground. This showed the importance of interventions for reforming and democratising the administration and the workplace, and for the related human resource development of the functionaries. Such interventions could greatly enrich and energise the development processes for effective and adequate fulfilment of the basic needs of the people, and for obtaining the human development goals of capability promotion and empowerment among them, and in civil society.

Notes

1. Address to the nation by Shri K.R. Narayanan, President of India, on the eve of Republic Day 2000, New Delhi.
2. *Ibid*. Also see Sen 1979, 1997 for discussion of 'equality for what'. For employment, poverty and new economic policies, see Chandoke 1998; Datt 1999; and Gupta 1999.
3. The President's Address to the nation, Republic Day 2000.
4. *Ibid.*
5. For discussion about the role of civil society in democracy and development, see Mahajan 1999a, 1999b; Ratliff 1999; and various contributions cited there. Also see Mehta (1998: 185–89).
6. The President's Address, Republic Day 2000.
7. *Ibid.*
8. Lack of vigilance can be seen in train accidents, fires at public places, in road transport, in health services, in functioning of schools, in fact, almost everywhere from escalator death to the episodes concerning the hijacking of the Indian Airlines Flight No. 814 in December 1999.

9. The Inquiry Committee which went into the escalator death (of a 13–year old child on 13 December 1999 at the IGI airport) came to the conclusion that 'these was poor supervision and monitoring work by the staff of the AAI'. For a report, see *The Times of India*, New Delhi, 8 February 2000. They were, thus, not only less vigilant but also insensitive to their functions.

10. For discussion of goals of development, see Mehta (1998: 102, 105–10), see Table 4.1 there.

11. For discussion of such behavioural tendencies, see Mehta (1998: 61–62).

12. The Parliament's Standing Committee for the Ministry of Human Resource Development has taken a serious note of attempts to 'saffronise' education and academic institutions. See a report by a special correspondent entitled 'Panel attacks attempts to "saffronise" education'. On-line edition of *The Hindu*, 29 March 2000.

13. The number of private aided and unaided schools has increased highly over the years. Thus, during 1993–94, there were in all 1,555,746 schools in the country of which 107,860 were private aided and 96,373 private unaided schools. See NCERT (1998: 3–4). At least some of these schools are known for their highly parochial 'management' and for their communal and authoritarian agenda.

14. For discussion, see a report titled 'Rout the Drought'. *The Sunday Observer*, 30 April–6 May 2000.

15. For the history of droughts and report on the current drought in the year 2000, see the cover story in *Outlook*, 8 May 2000.

16. For case studies of the success stories of traditional water harvesting system, and the apathy and negative attitudes of state functionaries in this respect, see Agarwal, Anil and Sunita Narain (eds.) 1997. Also, for an interesting discourse see Sethi 'Debating Drought'. *The Hindu* on-line edition, 4 May 2000.

17. See a report, 'Water as a Community Asset' by Mahesh Vijapurkar in *The Hindu* on India server, 19 April 2000.

18. Address to the nation by Shri K.R. Narayanan, President of India, on the occasion of the 50th Anniversary of the Republic of India from the Central Hall of Parliament, New Delhi, 27 January 2000. Also see Kothari 1988 for discussion of how the state works against democracy.

19. The recent action of the Central Vigilance Commissioner to publicise the names of the corrupt officials belonging to the Indian Administrative Service and the Indian Police Service on its website is a very welcome step in this direction. Much more is, however, needed as it is a deep-rooted structural problem. For some discussion, see Mehta (1998: 77–85).

20. For administrative reforms, see Mehta (1989a, 1998: 72–77); Potter 1986 and various contributions cited there.

The Centroid Loadings

Appendix-1

The Conservative Authoritarian Attitude Items

Item	Centroid Loading

Religionism

(1) It is necessary to be religious for a happy life.	0.566
(2) We should have full faith in religion and God.	0.544
(3) God has divided society into two classes—the rich and the poor.	0.457
(4) There is some supreme power above us and we should accept his decision without any reservation.	0.206
(5) It is the duty of the government to respect the privileges of the former princes.	0.458

Misanthropism

(6) Natural calamities can alone bring an end to social evils and personal quarrels.	0.496
(7) It is futile to hope that bad persons will be able to work with good persons.	0.476
(8) Western dress might look nice, but I do not like my family members wearing it.	0.386
(9) We should not mix too much with others because it produces mutual hatred.	0.340
(10) Family planning can never succeed in this country.	0.278
(11) Persons belonging to different religious groups will always find it difficult to work together.	0.312

Conservative Moralism

(12) Most problems of our country are due to our low
moral character.   0.469
(13) To whatever extent science may progress, certain
things can never be understood by the human brain.   0.468
(14) It is essential to use force against law-breakers.   0.320
(15) Nationalisation of large-scale industries is bound to lead
to inefficiency and loss.   0.571
(16) On deep thinking, we find that man works only for self-interest. 0.456
(17) Businessmen are more important than poets and writers
for society.   0.217
(18) Military training must be compulsory for every citizen of India. 0.183

Appendix-2

The Overall Modernity Items

Item	Centroid Loading

Openness

(1) Do you think a man can be truly good without having any religion at all? — 0.578

(2) If you were to meet a person who lives in another country a long way off, would you like his way of thinking? — 0.522

(3) How often do you get news and information from newspapers? — 0.364

(4) Which of the opinions do you agree with more? — 0.272

    (*a*) Some people say that it is necessary for a man and wife to limit the number of children to be born so that they can take better care of those they have.

    (*b*) Others say that is wrong for a man and wife to deliberately limit the number of children.

(5) Do you belong to any organisation, for example, social clubs, union, political groups or other groups? If 'yes', what are the names of these organisations you belong to? — 0.107

(6) What is more important for the future of a country? — 0.183

(7) Two 12-year old boys took time out from their work in the rice field. They were trying to figure out a way to grow same amount of rice with fewer hours of work. — 0.130

    (*a*) The father of one boy said: 'That is a good thing. Tell me your thoughts about how we should change our ways of growing rice.'

    (*b*) The father of other boys said: 'The way we have always done it. Talk about change, will only waste time.'

General Awareness

(8) Would you tell us what are the biggest problems facing the country? — 0.476

(9) Which of these kinds of news interests you the most? — 0.367

(10) Scientists in laboratories are studying such things as to what determines whether a baby is a boy or a girl and how it is that a seed turns into a plant. — 0.359

(11) If education is freely available, how much education do you think children of people like yourself should have? — 0.345

(12) What quality should a man have most to hold a high office? 0.307

(13) Did you get concerned, any time, with social problems such as communal riots? 0.302

Appendix-3

The Secularity Attitude Items

Item	Centroid Loading

Tolerance and Mutual Trust

(1) Seeing two students living together in a room: 0.448
   - (a) Some neighbours thought that they would soon quarrel, as one was Hindu and the other was Muslim.
   - (b) Some others thought that they could live together as friends despite different religions.

(2) One landlord gave his house on rent to some family of a different religion. Some neighbours made the following comments, which one appeals more to you?   0.480
   - (a) The landlord's religion will be polluted and for the sake of rent, he should not have given the house.
   - (b) The landlord is concerned with rent and not with the tenants' religion.

(3) Some new families started living in a locality dominated by a particular community. Two typical reactions of people were as follows, with which of the two do you agree?   0.547
   - (a) As different communities cannot live together in one locality, they should live in separate areas.
   - (b) People belonging to different castes, communities and religions should and can live together in one locality.

(4) 'Everyone, irrespective of caste and religion, must feel secured about his money and belongings'. How much do you agree or disagree with this statement?   0.476

(5) It is said that 'in our country the majority community should give protection to the minority communities'. How far do you agree or disagree with this statement?   0.485

(6) If a Hindu boy marries a Muslim girl, how should the parents behave?   0.231

(7) What can be the chief cause of conflict between two castes?   0.304

Equalitarianism

(8) All persons should get equal opportunity of employment irrespective of caste and religion.

(9) What do you think of a girl who marries a boy from a different community?   0.551

(10) In your opinion, what is more important for the progress of the country?   0.560
   (*a*) There should be one religion only.
   (*b*) All religions should get equal opportunity and freedom to develop.

(11) There is a famous temple in the city. Dalits and people of lower castes also want to go and worship there. What should the management do in such a situation?   0.319

(12) Which of the following two is a more appropriate thought: 0.480
   (*a*) One should love one's country even if one has to hate some other country.
   (*b*) Humanity is more important than the country, it is not good to hate others.

(13) If someone tells you that a theft took place in the neighbour-hood the previous night, how quickly would you believe it?   0.434

Appendix-4

The In-group–Out-group Attitude Items*

Scales	Centroid Loading
Kind–Cruel	0.717
Reliable–Unreliable	0.752
Honest–Dishonest	0.698
Good–Bad	0.635
Happy–Sad	0.762
Healthy–Unhealthy	0.796
Patriot–Traitor	0.713
Fair–Ugly	0.684
Loyal–Disloyal	0.635
One's own–Others	0.669

Note: *Social groups are to be rated on seven-point semantic scales.

Appendix Tables

Appendix Table 5.1
Loadings on Factor 1: Status Quoism in Development Functioning

Variables	Loading	h^2
Caste-like cadre mentality	0.65	0.82
Centralisation tendency	0.79	0.84
Number and target tendency	0.72	0.85
Reluctance to promote people's participation	0.79	0.86
Rentier-Dole tendency	0.70	0.76
Tokenism	0.87	0.92
Patronising manipulativeness	0.82	0.88
Other variable with significant loading on this factor:		
Facilitative problem-solving	−0.46	0.87

Appendix Table 5.2
Loadings on Factor 2: Capability Promoting–Dependency Inducing Tendency in Problem-solving

Variables	Loading	h^2
Directive style of dealing with development problems	−0.32	0.81
Prescriptive style of dealing with development problems	−0.85	0.87
Facilitative style of dealing with development problems	−0.79	0.87
Empowering style of dealing with development problems	−0.85	0.97
Pawn-inducing tendency	−0.81	0.93
Actor-promoting tendency	0.71	0.94
Other variable with significant loading on this factor:		
Sense of initiative and autonomy	0.54	0.84

Appendix Table 5.3
Loadings on Factor 3: Workplace Satisfaction

Variables	Loading	h^2
Perceived influence at the workplace	0.54	0.80
Perceived amenities	0.72	0.77
Perceived nature of job	0.76	0.91
Perceived supervisory behaviour	0.83	0.95
Other variables with significant loading on this factor:		
Prescriptive leadership style	−0.47	0.91
Directive style of dealing with development problems	0.72	0.81
Actor-promoting tendency	0.60	0.94

Appendix Table 5.4
Loadings on Factor 4: Motivating-Empowering Leadership Values (MOEM)

Variables	Loading	h^2
Directive leadership values/style	−0.43	0.82
Prescriptive leadership values/style	−0.76	0.91
Enabling leadership values/style	0.61	0.91
Dominative leadership values/style	−0.93	0.98
Integrative leadership values/style	0.93	0.98
Other variable with significant loading on this factor:		
Sense of initiative and autonomy	0.45	0.91

Appendix Table 5.5
Loadings on Factor 5: Sense of Personal Efficacy (SPE)

Variables	Loading	h^2
Sense of initiative and autonomy	0.72	0.84
Sense of self-esteem	0.85	0.80
Sense of reflective tendency	0.59	0.59
Sense of personal efficacy	0.96	0.98

Appendix Table 5.6
Loadings on Factor 6: Patronising-Educative Leadership Values/Style (PAED)

Variables	Loading	h^2
Educative leadership	0.80	0.85
Enabling leadership	−0.65	0.91
Other variable with significant loading on this factor:		
Perceived influence at the workplace	0.87	0.80

Appendix Table 5.7
Loadings on Factor 7: Dominative Leadership Values/Style (DOLS)

Variables	Loading	h^2
Directive leadership values/style	0.69	0.82
Other variable with significant loading on this factor:		
Caste-like cadre mentality	0.44	0.82

Appendix Table 5.8
Principal Component Factors in the Data Obtained from Group 1 (N = 40)

Rotated Factors (Varimax)	Eigen Value	Per cent of Variance	Cumulative Percentage	Mean h^2
(1) Status quoism in development functioning	4.75	21.6	21.6	0.71
(2) Workplace satisfaction (WPS)	3.50	15.9	37.5	0.75
(3) Dependency inducing-capability promoting tendency in problem-solving (DIT–CPT)	3.17	14.4	51.9	0.84
(4) Prescriptive-dominative leadership	1.61	7.3	59.2	0.80
(5) Dominative-empowering leadership (DOLE–MOEM)	1.35	6.2	65.4	0.87
(6) Sense of personal efficacy (SPE)	1.35	6.0	71.4	0.66
(7) Patronising-educative leadership values (PAED)	1.17	5.3	76.7	0.93

Appendix Table 5.9
Principal Component Factors in the Data Obtained from Group 2 (N = 40)

Rotated Factors (Varimax)	Eigen Value	Per cent of Variance	Cumulative Percentage	Mean h^2
(1) Status quoism in development functioning	4.09	18.6	18.6	0.70
(2) Workplace satisfaction (WPS)	3.05	13.9	32.5	0.76
(3) Tendency for centralisation	2.46	11.2	43.7	0.64
(4) Dependency inducing–Capability promoting tendency in problem-solving (DIT–CPT)	2.02	9.2	52.9	0.80
(5) Sense of personal efficacy (SPE)	1.84	8.4	61.2	0.68
(6) Dominative (DOLS) vs. motivating-empowering leadership values (MOEM)	1.55	7.0	68.2	0.86
(7) Patronising-educative leadership values (PAED)	1.16	5.3	73.5	0.79

Appendix Table 5.10
Principal Component Factors in Data Obtained from the Total Scores on Various Instruments (Constructs), Group 1 (**N = 40**)

Rotated Factors (Varimax)	Eigen value	Per cent of Variance	Cumulative Percentage	Mean h^2
(1) Capability promoting tendency in problem-solving	3.24	46.4	46.4	0.88
(2) Motivating-empowering leadership value (MOEM)	1.25	17.9	64.3	0.93
(3) Status quoism in development functioning	1.13	16.1	80.4	0.78

Other significant loadings on:

Factors

	1	2	3
Variable	CPT	MOEM	Status Quoism
Sense of efficacy	0.720		
Actor role		0.405	
Workplace satisfaction		0.443	0.567

Appendix Table 5.11
Assessment of Administrative Behaviour: Status Quoism vs. Change Proneness in Development Functioning

(Scale Validated in the Principal Component Factor Analysis, N = 80)

Variables	Loading on Factor 1	h^2
(1) Cadre mentality	0.43	0.48
(2) Centralisation tendency	0.63	0.57
(3) Number and target tendency	0.79	0.63
(4) Reluctance to people's participation	0.70	0.59
(5) Rentier-Dole tendency	0.71	0.62
(6) Tokenism: lack of interest in development	0.78	0.64
(7) Patronising manipulativeness	0.70	0.54

Appendix Table 5.12
Workplace Satisfaction Scale

(Scale Validated in Principal Component Factor Analysis, N = 80)

Variables	Loading on Factor 2	h^2
(1) Perceived influence at workplace	0.85	0.76
(2) Perceived amenities	0.76	0.61
(3) Perceived nature of job	0.85	0.74
(4) Perceived supervisory behaviour	0.80	0.68
Other measures with significant loading on this factor:		
Cadre mentality	0.34	0.48

Appendix Table 5.13
Dependency Inducing vs. Capability Promoting Tendency in Dealing with Development Problems

(Scale Validate in Principal Component Factor Analysis, N = 80)

Variables	Loading on Factor 3	h^2
(1) Directive style	0.39	0.47
(2) Prescriptive style	0.59	0.59
(3) Facilitative (educative) style	0.83	0.75
(4) Empowering style	−0.96	0.96
Other measures with significant loading on this factor:		
Centralisation tendency	−0.29	0.57

Appendix Table 5.14
Personal Efficacy Scale

(Scale Validated in Principal Component Factor Analysis, N = 80)

Variables	Loading on Factor 4	h^2
(1) Initiative	0.71	0.55
(2) Self-esteem	0.57	0.42
(3) Reflection	0.72	0.59
Other measures showing significant loading on this factor:		
Directive leadership values	−0.47	0.87
Directive style of problem-solving	−0.46	0.47
Prescriptive style of problem-solving	−0.30	0.59

Appendix Table 5.15
Motivating Empowering vs. Dominative Disempowering Leadership Values/Style

(Scale Validated in Principal Component Factor Analysis, N = 80)

Variables	Loading on Factor 5	h^2
(1) Directive leadership	0.35	0.43
(2) Prescriptive leadership	0.85	0.87
(3) Enabling leadership	−0.78	0.92

Appendix Table 5.16
Patronising-Educative Leadership Values/Style

(Scale Validated in Principal Component Factor Analysis, N = 80)

Variables	Loading on Factor 6	h^2
(1) Prescriptive leadership	−0.32	0.87
(2) Educative leadership	0.87	0.76
(3) Enabling leadership	−0.47	0.92
Other measures with significant loading on this factor:		
Caste-like Cadre mentality	0.39	0.48
'Prescriptive' style of dealing with development problems	0.26	0.59

Appendix Table 6.1
Dimensions in Leadership:
Mean Scores, Variations and Range of Scores

Leadership values/styles	Group 1 N = 40	Group 2 N = 40	Composite Group N = 80	Revised Scoring
Agricultural Extension Scientists/Officials				
Directive (DOLS)				
Mean	0.72	1.00	0.90	2.70*
SD	0.93	1.55	1.01	1.68
SE Mean	0.15	0.10	0.11	0.19
Range:				
Minimum	0	0	0	0
Maximum	3	5	5	6
Prescriptive				
Mean	1.47	2.00	1.77	–
SD	1.26	1.36	1.33	–
SE Mean	0.20	0.21	0.15	–
Range:				
Minimum	0	0	0	–
Maximum	6	6	6	–
Patronising-Educative (PAED)				
Mean	2.60	2.82	2.56	Same as
SD	1.47	1.24	1.30	before
SE Mean	0.23	0.20	0.14	
Range:				
Minimum	0	0	0	–
Maximum	6	6	6	–
Motivating-Empowering (MOEM)				
Mean	5.20	4.17	4.76	Same as
SD	1.77	1.77	1.91	before
SE Mean	0.28	0.28	0.21	
Range:				
Minimum	1	0	0	
Maximum	8	8	8	

Notes: *Includes the prescriptive style.

Appendix Table 6.2
Variables in Problem-solving Scale:
Mean Scores, Variations and Range of Scores

	Agricultural Extension Scientists/Officials			
Approach to Development Problem-solving	Group 1 $N = 40$	Group 2 $N = 40$	Composite Group $N = 80$	Revised Scoring
Directive (DOLS)				
Mean	0.49	0.52	0.54	
SD	0.74	0.75	0.76	
SE Mean	0.12	0.12	0.08	
Range:				
Minimum	0	0	0	
Maximum	3	3	3	
Prescriptive				
Mean	0.40	0.32	0.85	
SD	0.71	0.73	1.45	
SE Mean	0.11	0.11	0.16	
Range:				
Minimum	0	0	0	
Maximum	3	3	6	
Facilitative				
Mean	2.72	2.42	2.96	
SD	1.69	1.45	1.66	
SE Mean	0.27	0.23	0.19	
Range:				
Minimum	0	0	0	
Maximum	6	6	8	
Enabling				
Mean	6.47	6.72	6.07	
SD	2.28	2.19	2.10	
SE Mean	0.36	0.35	0.24	
Range:				
Minimum	1	1	1	
Maximum	9	9	10	
DIT–CPT (as per revised scoring)				
Mean				31.57
SD				3.72
SE Mean				0.42
Range:				
Minimum				24.00
Maximum				40.00

Appendix Table 6.3
Variables in Sense of Personal Efficacy:
Mean Scores, Variations and Range of Scores

Agricultural Extension Scientists/Officials			
Assessment of Development Functioning Variables/Tendencies	Group 1 N = 40	Group 2 N = 40	Combined Group N = 80
Initiative			
Mean	17.60	17.02	17.27
SD	2.11	2.59	2.36
SE Mean	0.33	0.41	0.26
Range:			
Minimum	14	12	12
Maximum	22	22	22
Self-esteem			
Mean	19.37	19.25	18.91
SD	2.24	2.42	2.46
SE Mean	0.35	0.38	0.27
Range:			
Minimum	13	13	13
Maximum	24	24	25
Reflective			
Mean	18.67	17.95	18.46
SD	2.55	2.63	2.59
SE Mean	0.40	0.41	0.29
Range:			
Minimum	13	13	13
Maximum	23	25	25
Sense of Personal Efficacy			
Mean	55.65	54.25	54.66
SD	4.94	5.51	5.27
SE Mean	0.78	0.87	0.59
Range:			
Minimum	43	43	43
Maximum	69	64	69

Appendix Table 6.4

Dimensions in Development Functioning:
Mean Scores, Variations and Range of Scores

Assessment of Development Functioning Variables/Tendencies	Agricultural Extension Scientists/Officials		
	Group 1 N = 40	Group 2 N = 40	Combined Group N = 80
Caste-like Cadre Mentality			
Mean	5.30	5.32	5.17
SD	1.38	1.42	1.37
SE Mean	0.22	0.22	0.15
Range:			
Minimum	3	3	3
Maximum	8	8	8
Centralisation			
Mean	5.82	6.15	5.83
SD	1.48	1.59	1.33
SE Mean	1.23	0.25	0.15
Range:			
Minimum	3	3	3
Maximum	11	11	11
Number and Target Tendency			
Mean	5.97	6.25	6.11
SD	1.67	1.66	1.53
SE Mean	0.26	0.26	0.17
Range:			
Minimum	3	3	3
Maximum	9	10	10
Reluctance to Promote People's Participation			
Mean	6.50	6.90	6.61
SD	1.91	1.72	1.78
SE Mean	0.30	0.27	0.20
Range:			
Minimum	3	3	3
Maximum	10	10	10
Rentier-Dole Tendency			
Mean	6.02	6.12	6.17
SD	1.79	1.38	1.73
SE Mean	0.28	0.21	0.19
Range:			
Minimum	3	3	3
Maximum	10	9	11

Tokenism

Mean	6.25	6.42	6.17
SD	1.64	1.64	· 1.50
SE Mean	0.26	0.26	0.17
Range:			
Minimum	3	3	3
Maximum	10	10	10

Patronising Manipulativeness

Mean	6.27	6.40	6.31
SD	1.57	1.46	1.66
SE Mean	0.25	0.23	0.18
Range:			
Minimum	3	3	3
Maximum	9	9	10

Combined Development Functioning

Mean	40.05	43.65	42.31
SD	8.64	8.16	7.35
SE Mean	1.37	1.29	0.84
Range:			
Minimum	21	21	21
Maximum	61	61	61

Appendix Table 6.5
Dimensions in Workplace Satisfaction:
Mean Scores, Variations and Range of Scores

	Agricultural Extension Scientists/Officials		
WPS Variables	Group 1 N = 40	Group 2 N = 40	Combined Group N = 80
Perceived Influence			
Mean	18.30	16.92	17.81
SD	3.96	4.93	4.41
SE Mean	0.63	0.78	0.49
Range:			
Minimum	12	8	8
Maximum	27	26	27
Perceived Amenities			
Mean	18.02	16.05	16.71
SD	3.85	4.22	4.05
SE Mean	0.61	0.67	0.45
Range:			
Minimum	9	8	8
Maximum	28	23	28
Perceived Nature of Job			
Mean	22.00	19.92	20.84
SD	3.02	4.30	4.03
SE Mean	0.48	0.68	0.45
Range:			
Minimum	14	8	8
Maximum	29	27	29
Perceived Supervisory Behaviour			
Mean	21.22	20.20	20.46
SD	3.29	3.73	3.74
SE Mean	0.52	0.59	0.42
Range:			
Minimum	14	13	11
Maximum	29	26	29
Workplace Satisfaction (WPS)			
Mean	79.70	73.10	79.91
SD	11.27	14.45	13.31
SE Mean	1.78	2.28	1.49
Range:			
Minimum	57	39	39
Maximum	113	97	113

Appendix Table 6.6
Motivational Needs:
Mean Scores and Other Related Data for Three Needs

Needs	Group 1 N = 40	Group 2 N = 40	Combined Group N = 80
Need for Personal Achievement			
Mean Score	4.37	4.35	4.36
SD	2.58	2.68	2.61
SE Mean	0.408	0.425	0.292
Range:			
Minimum	0	0	0
Maximum	10	11	11
Need for Social Achievement			
Mean Score	2.47	2.75	2.61
SD	2.6	2.81	2.70
SE Mean	0.413	0.444	0.320
Range:			
Minimum	0	0	0
Maximum	12	13	13
Need for Influence			
Mean Score	3.95	4.10	4.09
SD	2.09	2.44	2.26
SE Mean	0.330	0.385	0.252
Range:			
Minimum	0	0	0
Maximum	8	10	10

Notes: *For scoring system, see Mehta (1994a; Appendix-1).

Appendix Table 6.7
Socio-psychological Monitoring:
Instrumentation—Inventory of Scales and Variables

Variable (V)

Personal Background: Codes

V1 Sex (Male = 1, Female = 2)

V2 Age (upto 30 = 1, 30–40 = 2, above 40 = 3)

V3 Employer (State = 1, ICAR = 2)

Leadership Behaviour

V4 Dominative Leadership

V5 Prescriptive Leadership

V6 Educative Leadership

V7 Enabling Leadership

V8 Dominative (V4–V5) Leadership

V9 Integrative (V6–V7) Leadership

Styles of Dealing with Development Problems

V10 Directive Style of Dealing with Development Problems

V11 Prescriptive Style of Dealing with Development Problems

V12 Facilitating Style of Dealing with Development Problems

V13 Empowering Style of Dealing with Development Problems

V14 Inducing 'Pawn' Role (V10+V11)

V15 Promoting 'Actor Role' (V12+V13)

Sense of Efficacy

V16 Autonomy vs. Dependency

V17 Self-esteem vs. Self-Depreciation

V18 Reflective vs. Repetitive Behaviour

V19 Efficacy vs. Powerlessness (V16+V17+V18)

Systemic Tendencies: Assessing Development Functioning

V20 Caste-like Cadre Mentality

V21 Centralisation Tendency

V22 Number and Target Tendency

V23 Reluctance to Promote People's Participation

V24 Rentier-Dole Tendency

V25 Tokenism: Lack of Interest in Development

V26 Patronising Manipulativeness

V27 Total (V20+V21+22+V23+V24+V25+V26): Assessment of Development Functioning

Workplace Satisfaction vs. Alienation

V28 Perceived Influence at the Workplace

V29 Perceived Amenities at the Workplace

V30 Perceived Nature of Job

V31 Perceived Supervisory Behaviour at the Workplace

V32 Total (V28+V29+V30+V31): Workplace Satisfaction vs. Workplace Alienation

Appendix Table 6.8
Explaining Variance in Problem-solving Behaviour, * (N = 80)

Independent Variables	Directive Tendency		Prescriptive Tendency		Facilitative Tendency		Enabling Tendency		DIT–CIT	
	Beta	Sig	Beta	Sig	Beta	Sig	Beta	Sig	Beta	Sig
Perceived supervisory behaviour at the workplace	–0.35	0.009	–	–	–	–	–	–	–	–
Rentier-Dole tendency	0.29	0.005	–	–	–	–	–	–	–	–
Reflective efficacy	–0.25	0.01	–	–	–	–	–	–	–	–
Perceive influence at the workplace	0.24	0.06	–	–	–	–	–	–	–	–
Motivating-empowering leadership values (MOEM)	–	–	–0.32	0.004	–	–	–	–	–	–
Perceived nature of job (NJ)	–	–	0.22	0.04	–	–	–	–	–	–
Sex (1 for M, 2 for F)	–	–	–	–	–0.30	0.007	–	–	–	–
Dominative leadership values/style (DOLS)	–	–	–	–	–	–	–0.28	0.01	–0.33	0.003
Self-esteem	–	–	–	–	–	–	–	–	0.20	0.06
Reluctance to promote people's participation	–	–	–	–	–	–	–	–	–0.18	0.08
R Square	0.23		0.13		0.09		0.08		0.11	
Adjusted R Square	0.20		0.11		0.08		0.07		0.10	
Standard error	0.680		0.684		1.60		2.11		3.53	
F	7.79		5.90		7.61		6.60		9.57	
Significance of F	0.0001		0.004		0.007		0.012		0.003	

Notes: *Results in Appendix Tables 6.8 to 6.11 are derived by stepwise multiple regression analysis, here criteria or PIN = 0.0500 and POUT = 0.100 were used for inclusion or exclusion of the given independent variables in the equation. Some variables with PIN somewhat higher than 0.05 are shown in these tables because of their research significance. The contri-bution of such variables to variance in the given independent variable is, however, not included in the R square values.

Appendix Table 6.9
Explaining Variance in Leadership Values/Style, (N = 80)

Independent Variables	Dominative Leadership (DOLS)		Patronising- Educative Leadership (PAED)		Motivating- Empowering Leadership (MOEM)	
	Beta	Sig	Beta	Sig	Beta	Sig
Capability promoting (enabling approach)	–0.29	0.008	–	–	–	–
Employer (1 for state, 2 for ICAR)	–0.27	0.013	0.20	0.06	–	–
Amenities at workplace	–0.19	0.07	–	–	0.27	0.01
Age	0.21	0.06	–	–	–	–
Gender (1 for M, 2 for F)	–	–	0.30	0.007	–	–
Prescriptive DPS	–	–	–	–	–0.32	0.002
Need for influence	–	–	–	–	–0.24	0.02
R Square	0.150		0.089		0.211	
Adjusted R Square	0.128		0.077		0.179	
Standard Error	1.57		1.26		1.74	
F	6.78		7.58		6.76	
Significance of F	0.001		0.007		0.0004	

Appendix Table 6.10
*Explaining Variance in Sense of Personal Efficacy (Self-Concept)
and Workplace Satisfaction, (N = 80)*

Independent Variables	Sense of Personal Efficacy (Self-Concept)		Workplace Satisfaction	
	Beta	Sig	Beta	Sig
Directive problem-solving	–0.33	0.001	–	–
Employer (1 for state, 2 for ICAR)	–0.29	0.006	–	–
Cadre mentality	–	–	0.30	0.008
R Square	0.19		0.09	
Adjusted R Square	0.17		0.08	
Standard Error	4.81		12.79	
F	9.06		7.49	
Significance of F	0.0003		0.008	

Appendix Table 6.11
Explaining Variance in Motivational Needs, **(N = 80)**

Independent Variables	Need for Personal Achievement		Need for Social Achievement		Need for Influence	
	Beta	Sig	Beta	Sig	Beta	Sig
Employer (1 for state and 2 for ICAR)	0.43	0.0001	–	–	–	–
Need for influence	–0.26	0.009	–	–	–	–
Tendency for central- isation in development	–	–	0.37	0.004	–	–
Tokenism in development functioning	–	–	–0.29	0.02	–	–
Need for personal achieve- ment	–	–	–	–	–0.30	0.006
Motivating-empowering leader- ship values (MOEM)	–	–	–	–	–0.21	0.056
R Square	0.26		0.11		0.09	
Adjusted R Square	0.24		0.09		0.08	
Standard Error	2.28		2.57		2.16	
F	13.22		4.97		7.85	
Significance of F	0.0000		0.009		0.006	

Appendix Table 6.12
Mean Scores of High and Low Groups on Cadre Mentality

Group	Cadre Mentality	N	Cadre Mean	Standard Deviation	Standard Error
Group 1	Low	23	3.56	0.73	0.15
Group 2	High	57	5.82	0.98	0.13

Notes: Pooled Variance Estimate: t Value = –9.45, P = 0.000.
Separate Variance Estimate: t Value = –11.29, P = 0.000.

Appendix Table 6.13
Tendency for Centralisation in Development Functioning by Cadre Mentality

Group	Cadre Mentality	N	Centralisation Mean Score	Standard Deviation	Standard Error
Group 1	Low	23	5.26	1.14	0.24
Group 2	High	57	6.07	1.35	0.18

Notes: Pooled Variance Estimate: t Value = –2.54, P = 0.013.
Separate Variance Estimate: t Value = –2.73, P = 0.009.

Appendix Table 6.14
Status Quoism in Development Functioning by Cadre Mentality

Group	Cadre Mentality	N	Status Quoism Mean Score	Standard Deviation	Standard Error
Group 1	Low	23	39.30	6.73	1.40
Group 2	High	57	43.52	7.55	1.00

Notes: Pooled Variance Estimate: t Value = −2.33, P = 0.022.
Separate Variance Estimate: t Value = −2.45, P = 0.018.

Appendix Table 6.15
Perceived Influence at Workplace by Cadre Mentality

Group	Cadre Mentality	N	Perceived Influence Mean Score	Standard Deviation	Standard Error
Group 1	Low	23	16.30	4.58	0.95
Group 2	High	57	18.42	4.24	0.56

Notes: Pooled Variance Estimate: t Value = −1.97, P = 0.052.
Separate Variance Estimate: t Value = −1.91, P = 0.064.

Appendix Table 6.16
Perceived Amenities at Workplace by Cadre Mentality

Group	Cadre Mentality	N	Perceived Amenities Mean Score	Standard Deviation	Standard Error
Group 1	Low	23	14.96	3.65	0.76
Group 2	High	57	17.42	4.01	0.53

Notes: Pooled Variance Estimate: t Value = −2.55, P = 0.013.
Separate Variance Estimate: t Value = −2.66, P = 0.011.

Appendix Table 6.17
Perceived Supervisory Behaviour by Cadre Mentality

Group	Cadre Mentality	N	SB Mean Score	Standard Deviation	Standard Error
Group 1	Low	23	19.30	4.04	0.84
Group 2	High	57	20.93	3.54	0.47

Notes: Pooled Variance Estimate: t Value = −1.78, P = 0.078.
Separate Variance Estimate: t Value = −1.69, P = 0.100.

Appendix Table 6.18
Overall Workplace Satisfaction by Cadre Mentality

Group	Cadre Mentality	N	WPS Mean Score	Standard Deviation	Standard Error
Group 1	Low	23	70.52	13.19	2.75
Group 2	High	57	78.09	12.83	1.70

Notes: Pooled Variance Estimate: t Value = –2.37, P = 0.020.
Separate Variance Estimate: t Value = –2.34, P = 0.024.

References

Acharya, Poromesh (1996) 'Popular Education in India', in T.V. Sathyamurthy (1996a). pp. 388–409.

Adorno, T.W. et al. (1950) *The Authoritarian Personality*. New York: Harper and Brothers.

Agarwal, Anil and **Sunita Narain** (eds.) (1997) *Dying Wisdom*. New Delhi: Centre for Science and Environment.

Alatas, S.H. (1977) *The Myth of the Lazy Native*. London: Frank Cass.

Alexander, Jaffrey, C. (ed.) (1998) *Real Civil Societies: Dilemmas of Institutionalisation*. New Delhi: Sage.

Allport, G.W. (ed.) (1958) *The Nature of Prejudice*. New York: Doubleday, Anchor Books.

Almond, A.G. and **Sidney, Verba** (1963) *The Civic Culture: Political Attitudes and Democracy in Five Nations*. Princeton, N.J.: Princeton University Press.

Anant, S.S. (1972) *The Changing Concept of Caste in India*. New Delhi: Vikas Publications.

Anderson, C.A. (1966) 'The Modernization of Education', in M. Weiner (1996).

Auti, V.B. and **A.S. Chousalkar.** (1986). 'Nature and Political Ideas of Jyotirao Phule', in Karlekar and Chousalkar (eds.) *Ideas, Movements and Politics in India*. Kolhapur: Ajab Pustakalaya. pp. 9–25.

Bakshi, Rajni (1996) 'Development, Not Destruction: Alternative Politics in the Making', *Economic and Political Weekly* (EPW), 3 Feb: 255–57.

Basham, A.L. (1990) *The Origins and Development of Classical Hinduism*. Delhi: Oxford University Press.

Baviskar, Amita (1997) 'Tribal Politics and Discourse of Environmentalism', *Contributions to Indian Sociology*, 31: 195–223.

Bhan, Susheela (1995) 'Communal Exclusivism and Patterns of Social Interaction: A Study of Hindu and Muslim Students Youth', *Man and Development*, 17(4): 85–103.

Bhatty, Kiran (1998) 'Educational Deprivation in India: A Survey of Field Investigations', *EPW*, 27(4–10 July): 1731–40.

Bhusan, L.I. (1967) 'Personal Factors in Authoritarianism', *Journal of Psychological Researches*, 2(3): 119–25.

Bronfenbrenner, U. (1958) 'Socialisation and Social Class through Time and Space' in E.E. MacCoby et al. (eds.). *Readings in Social Psychology*. New York: Holt, Rinehart & Winston. pp. 400–25.

———— (1962) 'Soviet Methods of Character Education', *American Psychologist*, 17: 550–64.

Buch, M.B. and **M.R. Santhanam** (eds.) (1970) *Communication in Classroom*. Baroda: Centre for Advanced Study in Education.

Cattle, R. (1942) 'The Concept of Social Status', *Journal of Social Psychology*, 15: 293–308.

Chakravorty, S. (1987) *Development Planning–The Indian Experience*. Oxford: Clarendon Press.

Chandra, Sri (1967), 'Stereotypes of University Students Toward Different Ethnic Groups', *The Journal of Social Psychology*, 72(1): 87–94.

Chandra, Vipin (1987) *Communalism in Modern India*. Second Edition. New Delhi: Vikas Publishing House.

Chandoke, Neera (1998) 'The Assertion of Civil Society Against the State' in Mohanty et al. (1998). pp. 29–43.

Chang, H.J. and **R. Rowthorn** (eds.) (1995) *Role of the State in Economic Change*. Oxford: Clarendon Press.

Chattopadhyaya, D. (1989) *In Defence of Materialism in Ancient India*. New Delhi: People's Publishing House.

———— (1990) *The Global Philosophy for Every Man: Beginnings*. Bangalore: Navkarnataka.

Chauhan, B.R. (1955) 'Recent Trends among the Depressed Classes in Rajasthan', *Agra: University Journal of Research*, 3: 1558–61.

Coleman, J.S. (1965) *Education and Development*. Princeton N.J.: Princeton University Press.

Christie, R. and **M. Jahoda** (1966) *Studies in the Scope and Method of the Authoritarian Personality*. Glencoe, Illinois: The Free Press.

Datt, Gaurav (1999) 'Has Poverty Declined Since Economic Reforms?', *EPW*, 34(50): 3516–18.

Dean, T. (1999) 'New Millennium Will See One Billion Illiterates', *Free Press Journal*,

Deane, P. (1989) *State and the Economic System*. Oxford: Oxford University Press.

Desai, A.R. (1986) *Agrarian Struggles in India After Independence*. Delhi: Oxford University Press.

Devi, G. (1968) 'Sex Differences in Linguistic Stereotypes Among University Students', *Psychological Studies*, 13(2): 85–93.

Dreze, Jean and **Amartya Sen** (1995) *India: Economic Development and Social Opportunity*. Delhi: Oxford University Press.

Dube, S.C. (1974) *Contemporary India and Its Modernization*. New Delhi: Vikas Publishing House.

Dunn, S. and **E. Dunn** (1962) 'Directed Cultural Change in Soviet Russia', *American Anthropologist*, 64: 328–39.

Elias, N. and **J.L. Scotson** (1965) *The Established and the Outsiders*. London: Frank Cass.

EPW (1999) 'Positive Verdict', Editorial Comment, *EPW*, 34(41): 2891–92.

Engineer, Asghar Ali (1998) 'Srikrishna Commission Report: Painstaking Documentation', *EPW*, 33(33 and 34): 2215–16.

Evans, Peter (1987) 'Class, State, and Dependence in East Asia: Lessons for Latin Americanists', in Frederic C. Deyo (ed.), *The Political Economy of the New Asian Industrialism*. Ithaca, NY and London: Cornell University Press.

———— (1996) 'Government Action, Social Capital and Development: Creating Synergy Across the Public-Private Divide', *World Development*, 24(6) special section.

Frank, Andre Gunder (1998) *ReORIENT: Global Economy in the Asian Age*. New Delhi: Vistaar Publications.

Freire, Paulo (1972) *Pedagogy of the Oppressed*. Marmondsworth: Penguin Books.

Ganguli, H.C. (1972) 'Prejudice and its Social Consequences', *Indian Journal of Social Work*, 33(3): 243.

Gautam, M.L. (1970) 'Secularism and University Students', *Social Welfare*, 16(12): 13–14.

George, E.I. and **M. George** (1970) 'Communal Stereotypes in Kerala', *Journal of Psychological Researches*, 14(1): 135–42.

Ghurye, G.S. (1957) *Caste and Class in India*. Bombay: Popular Prakashan.

——— (1968) *Social Tension in India*. Bombay: Popular Prakashan.

Gore, M.S. (1993) *The Social Context of an Ideology–Ambedkar's Political and Social Thoughts*. New Delhi: Sage.

Government of India (1966) Education and National Development. Report of the Education Commission 1964–66. New Delhi: Ministry of Education.

——— (1974) *Education in India*. New Delhi: Ministry of Education.

Gupta, Dipankar (1997) 'Civil Society in the Indian Context', *Contemporary Sociology*, 26(3): 125–34.

——— (1999) 'Survivors in Survivals: Reconciling Citizenship and Cultural Particularisms', *EPW*, 34(33): 2313–23.

Gupta, S.P. (1999) 'Trickle Down Theory Revisited: The Role of Employment and Poverty'. Lecture delivered at the Annual Conference of the Indian Society of Labour Economics. 17–19 November.

Gusfield, J.R. (1967) 'Tradition and Modernity: Misplaced Polarities in the Study of Social Change', *American Journal of Sociology*, 72(4): 351–62.

Hess, R.P. and **David Easten** (1962), 'The Role of Elementary School in Political Socialization', *The School Review*, 70: 257–65.

Himmelweit, H. (1957) 'Social Class Differences in Parent–Child Relations in England' in N. Anderson (ed.), *Studies of Family*, 2. Gottingen: Vadenhoeck and Rupreeht.

Hobsbawm, E. (1994) *The Age of Extremes–A History of the World*, 1914–1998. New York: Pantheon Books.

Holes, H.W. (1951) 'The Civic Education Project of Cambridge', *Phi Delta Koean*, 33: 168–71.

Hollingshead, A.B. and **C.R. Fredrick** (1958) *Social Class and Mental Illness*. New York: Wiley & Sons.

Hommond, P.E. (1966) 'Secularization, Incorporation and Social Relations', *American Journal of Sociology*, 72(2): 188–94.

Hyman, Herbert H. (1959) *Political Socialization: A Study in the Psychology of Politics*. New York: The Free Press.

IPHRC (Indian People's Human Rights Commission) (1993) 'The People's Verdict: An Inquiry into the December '92 and January '93 Riots in Bombay'. Bombay: IPHRC.

Inkeles, Alex (1966) 'The Modernization of Man' in Weiner (1996).

Inkeles, Alex and **D.H. Smith** (1974) *Becoming Modern*. Cambridge, MA: Harvard Press.

Inkeles, Alex and **A.K. Singh** (1968), 'A Cross Cultural Measure of Modernity and Some Popular Indian Images', *Journal of General and Applied Psychology*, 1(1): 33–43.

Issack, H.R. (1964) *India's Ex-untouchables*. New York: John Day.

Javeed, Alam (1999) 'What is Happening Inside Indian Demography?', *EPW*, 34(37): 2649–56.

Kahl, J.A. (1968) *The Measurement of Modernism*. Austin: University of Texas Press.

Kanta, P. (1953) 'Stereotypes and Newspapers'. Unpublished Master's Thesis in Psychology, University of Lucknow.

Kerlinger, Fred N. (1978) *Foundations of Behavioural Research*. Delhi: Surjeet Publications.

Kohli, Atul (1987) *The State and Poverty in India: The Politics of Reform.* Cambridge: Cambridge University Press.

Kohli, Atul (1994) 'Centralization and Powerlessness: India's Democracy in a Comparative Perspective', in J. Migdal, A. Kohli and V. Shue (eds.), *State Power and Social Forces–Domination and Transformation in the Third World.* Cambridge: Cambridge University Press.

Kohn, Melvin (1969) *Class and Conformity: A Study in Values.* Illinois: The Dorsey Press.

Kothari, Rajni (1970) *Politics in India.* New Delhi: Orient Longman.

───── (1971) 'More Opposition', *Seminar*, 137: 22–27.

───── (1988) *State Against Democracy: In Search of Human Governance.* Delhi: Ajanta.

Kozul-Wright, R. (1995) 'The Myth of Anglo-Saxon Capitalism: Reconstructing the History of the American State' in H.J. Chang and R. Rowthorn (1995).

Krauss, Irring (1964) 'Educational Aspiration Among Working Class Youth', *American Sociological Review*, 29: 867–79.

Kretch, K. et al. (1962) *Individual in Society.* New York: McGraw Hill.

Krishna, Sumi (1996) 'The Appropriation of Dissent: The State vis-à-vis People's Movements' in T.V. Sathyamurthy (1996a). pp. 238–57.

Kumar, Krishna (1998) 'Education and Society in Post-Independence India: Looking Towards the Future', *EPW*, 34(23): 1391–96.

Kumar, Ravinder (1986) *Essays in the Social History of Modern India.* Delhi: Oxford University Press.

Kuppuswamy, B. (1962) *The Socio-economic Status Scale.* New Delhi: Manasayan.

Langton, K.P. (1969) *Political Socialization.* London: Oxford University Press.

Leftwich, Adrian (1995) 'Bringing Politics Back In: Towards a Model of the Developmental State', *Journal of Development Studies*, 31(3).

Lieten, G.K. (1996) *Development, Devolution and Democracy: Village Discourse in West Bengal.* New Delhi: Sage.

Lipset, S.M. (1960) *Political Man: The Social Bases of Politics.* London: Heinemann.

Lynch, Owen M. (1969) *The Politics of Untouchability: Social Change.* New York: Columbia University Press.

Mahajan, Gurpreet (1999a) 'Civil Society and Its Avtars: What Happened to Freedom and Democracy?', *EPW*, 34(20): 1188–96.

───── (1999b) 'Civil Society, State and Democracy', *EPW*, 34(49): 3471–2.

Mahar, Michael J. (ed.) (1972) *The Untouchables in Contemporary India.* Phoenix: The University of Arizona Press.

McClelland, D.C. and **D.C. Winter** (1969) *Motivating Economic Achievement.* New York: The Free Press.

Mehta, Prayag (1967/68) *Understanding Classroom Behaviour: A Manual.* New Delhi: NCERT.

───── (1969) *Achievement Motive in High School Boys.* New Delhi: NCERT.

───── (1971a) 'Some Perceived Needs and Problems of University Youth' in P. Mehta (1971b). pp. 30–48.

───── (ed.) (1971b) *Indian Youth: Emerging Problems and Issues.* Bombay: Somaya Publications.

───── (1975a) 'School and Ideology: Role of School Management in Social Learning of Children'. Unpublished Report.

───── (1975b) *Election Campaign: Anatomy of Mass Influence.* New Delhi: National Publishing House.

Mehta, Prayag (1975c) *Efficacy, Participation and Politics.* Unpublished Manuscript. New Delhi: PADC.

—— (1975d) 'Development of Efficacy in Working People', *National Labour Institute Bulletin,* 1: 7–9.

—— (1976a) *Managing Motivation in Education.* Ahmedabad: Sahitya Mudernalaya.

—— (1976b) 'From Economism to Democratic Commitment: The Role of Workers' Participation', *Vikalpa,* 1(4): 39–46.

—— (1976c) 'Analysing Imagery for Social Efficacy'. Mimeo. New Delhi: National Labour Institute.

—— (1976d) 'The Alienated Middle Managers', *NLI Bulletin,* 3: 95–96.

—— (1977a) 'Efficacy, Participation and Politics', *ICSSR Research Abstract Quarterly,* 6(3–4): 88–89.

—— (1977b) 'Employee Motivation and Work Satisfaction in Public Enterprise', *Vikalpa,* 2(3): 233–36.

—— (1978) 'Objective and Subjective Factors in Employee-Satisfaction in Life and Work', *Indian Journal of Industrial Relations,* 2(3): 433–44.

—— (1981) 'Political Processes and Behaviour' in Udai Pareek (ed.) *A Survey of Research in Psychology,* 1971–76, Part II: 577–615. New Delhi: ICSSR and Popular Prakashan.

—— (1983) 'Political Efficacy and Participation in Socio-economic Development', *Journal of Rural Development,* 2(6): 563–70.

—— (1989a) *Bureaucracy, Organisational Behaviour and Development.* New Delhi: Sage.

—— (1989b) *Participation and Organisation Development.* Jaipur: Rawat.

—— (1992) '*Movement for Total Literacy: The Case of Sonebhadra*'. Mimeo. New Delhi: PADC.

—— (1994a) 'New Economic Policy, Workplace and Human Development', *EPW,* 29(22): M75–82.

—— (1994b) 'Empowering the People for Social Achievement' in R. Kanungo and Mendonca Manuel (eds.) *Work Motivation: Models for Developing Countries.* New Delhi: Sage. pp. 161–83.

—— (1994c) *Social Achievement Motivation: Needs, Values and Work Organization.* New Delhi: Concept Publishing Co.

—— (1995) *Education, Participation and Empowerment: Studies in Human Development.* New Delhi: Concept Publishing Co.

—— (1996a) 'Human Development Performance in India: State Functioning and Management of Programmes', *Man and Development,* 18(2): 72–95.

—— (1996b) 'Gender Issues in Population Planning: Content Analysis of Ideas Generated at a National Seminar', CRRID, Chandigarh.

—— (1998) *A Psychological Strategy for Alternative Human Development: India's Performance Since Independence.* New Delhi: Sage.

—— (1999) 'Identification of Training and Development Needs in a State Mines and Minerals Enterprise', Unpublished Report. New Delhi: PADC.

—— (2000) 'Human Development in South Asian Countries: Economic Policy, Work and Human Welfare'. Paper presented at the Seminar on India at the Threshold of a New Millennium: The Unfinished Agenda and Challenges Ahead, CRRID, Chandigarh. January.

—— (forthcoming) *Theory and Practice of Development: Lessons from Some Case Studies.* New Delhi: Participation and Development Centre.

Mehta, Prayag, Gera, K., and **M.L. Rao** (1974) Understanding Communal Behaviour. Unpublished Monograph, Psychology Department, University of Udaipur.

Mehta, Prayag and **T.V. Rao** (1973) 'Classroom Interaction Analysis: A Report of Research and Training in India', *Indian Educational Review*, 8: 1–15.

Merton, Robert K. (1959) *Social Theory and Social Structure.* New York: The Free Press.

Migdal, Joel S., (1994) 'The State in Society: An Approach to Struggles for Domination', in J. Migdal, A. Kohli, and V. Shue (eds.). *State Power and Social Forces–Denomination and Transformation in the Third World.* Cambridge: Cambridge University Press.

Misra, R.K. (1962) 'Caste Stereotypes: A Socio-Psychological Analysis of Attitudes and Images'. Unpublished Ph.D. thesis. University of Lucknow.

Mohanty, G.S. and I. Singh (1966) 'A Study of Authoritarianism Among Service Officers and its Relationship to Various Measures of Personality, *Indian Journal of Psychology*, 41(3): 33–36.

Mohanty, Manoranjan (1995) 'The Concept of Empowerment', *EPW*, 17 June: 1434–36.

——— (1998) 'Social Movements in Creative Society: Of Autonomy and Interconnection' in Mohanty, et al. (1998).

Mohanty, Manoranjan, P.N. Mukherjee and **Olle Tomquist** (eds.) (1998) *People's Rights: Social Movements and the State in the Third World.* New Delhi: Sage.

Mouzelis, Nicos (1990) *Post Marxist Alternatives: Contraction of Social Order.* London: MacMillan.

Mukherjee, R. et al. (1951) *Inter Caste Tension: Survey under the Auspices of the UNESCO.* Lucknow: Lucknow University.

Murphy, Gardner (1953) *In the Minds of Men: The Study of Human Behaviour and Social Tension in India.* New York: Basic Books Inc..

Murphy, Lois B. (1953) *Depressed and Oppressed.* New Delhi: S. Chand & Co.

Murthy, K.G., Krishna Rao and **G. Lakshmana** (1969) 'Socio-economic and Demographic Factors and Voting Behaviour', *Political Science Review*, 81(2): 193–213.

Naik, J.P. (1965) *Educational Planning in India.* New Delhi: Allied Publishers.

——— (1972) 'Education of the Scheduled Castes'. New Delhi: Occasional ICSSR Monograph (6).

Narain, Iqbal (1972) 'Rural Local Politics and Primary School Management' in S.H. Rudolph and L.I. Rudolph (eds.) *Education and Politics in India,* New Delhi: Oxford University Press. pp.148–64.

National Council of Educational Research and Training (1961), 'Education and Democratic Attitude in School', *Investigations*, Vol. 1. New Delhi: NCERT.

——— (1998), *Sixth All India Educational Survey: School and Physical Facilities,* Vol. 2. New Delhi: NCERT.

National Education Association (1940) *Learning Ways of Democracy: A Case Book in Civics.* USA Education Politics Commission. Washington: NEA.

Natraj, S. (1959) *A Century of Social Reform in India.* Bombay: Asia Publishing House.

Neugarten, B.L. (1946) 'Social Class and Friendship among School Children', *American Sociological Review*, 51: 305–13.

Nomani, Rashid (1968) 'An Analysis of the Content of Some Social Studies Textbooks in the Light of the Concept of Secularism', *Journal of Educational Research and Extension*, 5(2): 78–80.

North, Douglass C. (1990) *Institutions, Institutional Change and Economic Performance.* Cambridge University Press.

Oad, L.K. (1989) 'Primary Education under Panchayati Raj: A Case Study in P.R. Panchamukhi (ed.) *Studies in Educational Reforms in India,* 2: 105–206. Bombay: Himalaya.

Omvedt, Gail (1986) 'Caste, Agrarian Relations and Agrarian Conflicts' in A.R. Desai (1986). pp. 168–95.

——— (1994) *Reinventing Revolution: New Social Movements and Socialist Tradition in India.* New York: Sharp.

——— (1998) 'Peasant, Dalits and Women: Democracy and India's New Social Movements' in Mohanty et al. (1998). pp. 223–41.

Osgood, C.E. et al. (1957) *The Measurement of Meaning.* Illinois: University of Illinois Press.

Oughton, A. (1997) 'Competitiveness Policy in 1990s', *The Economic Journal,* 107(Sept): 1486–1503.

Pareek, U. (1971) *Directory of Indian Behavioural Science Research.* Delhi: Acharan Sahkar.

Parekh, Bhiku (1989) *Colonialism, Tradition and Reform: An Analysis of Gandhiji's Political Discourse.* New Delhi: Sage.

Parsons, Talcott (1959) 'The School Class as a Social System: Some of its Functions in American Society', *Harvard Educational Review,* 34: 297–318.

Portes, Alenjandro (1973) 'The Factorial Structure of Modernity: Empirical Relationships and Critique', *American Journal of Sociology,* 79(1): 15–44.

Potter, David C. (1986) *India's Political Administrators.* Oxford: Clarendon Press.

Prasad, J. (1953) Group Involvement in the Causation of Group Tension, *Indian Journal of Psychology,* 28: 1–14.

Przeworski, Adam et al. (1995) *Sustainable Democracy.* Cambridge: Cambridge University Press.

Pushpendra (1999) 'Dalit Assertion through Electoral Politics', *EPW,* 34(36): 206–18.

Putnam, Robert (1993) *Making Democracy Work: Civic Tradition in Modern Italy.* Princeton NJ: Princeton University Press.

Pylee, M. (1965) *Constitutional Government in India.* Bombay: Asia Publishing House.

Radhakrishanan, Sarvepalli (1940) *Eastern Religions and Western Thought.* Second Edition. New York: Oxford University Press.

Ram, Paras (1955) *A UNESCO Study of Social Tension in Aligarh, 1950–51.* Ahmedabad: New Order Book Co.

Ramnathan, G. (1965) *Educational Planning and National Integration.* Bombay: Asia Publishing House.

Ranchi Riot Enquiry Commission (1967–71) Report of the Ranchi Riots, Patna.

Rao, Hanumantha (1995) 'Structural Adjustments, Markets and the Poor', in Economic Policies, Development and Social Justice: Proceedings of AITUC Workshop, New Delhi: AITUC. 22–24 March, pp. 31–49.

Rao, M.L. and **Prayag Mehta** (1978) 'Measuring Implicit and Manifest Authoritarianism: Development and Standardisation of Tools', *Psychological Studies,* 23(1): 10–18.

Rao, M.L. and **Prayag Mehta** (1979) 'Communal Canker in Education: A Comparative Study of School and Family Environment', *Indian Educational Review,* April: 75–87.

Rath, R. and **N.C. Sarkar** (1960) 'Intercaste Relationship as Reflected in the Study of Attitude and Opinion of Six Hindu Caste Groups', *Journal of Social Psychology*, 15: 3–25.

Ratliff, William (1999) 'Development and Civil Society in Latin America and Asia', *ANNALS*, 565(Sept): 91–112.

Rawls, John (1971) *A Theory of Justice*. Cambridge: The Belknap Press of the Harvard University.

Reza, Kamalian (1999) 'Motivation, Values and Organisation Climate: A Study of Iranian Managers'. A doctoral thesis submitted at the Faculty of Management Studies, University of Delhi.

Roy, Ramashray (1971) 'A Study of 1969 Mid-term Elections in four States', *ICSSR Research Abstract Quarterly*, 5: 36–45.

Rueschemeyer, D.D., E. Huber-Stephens and **J.D Stephens** (1992) *Capitalist Development and Democracy*. Cambridge: Polity Press.

Sachs, Ignacy (1998) 'The State and the Social Partners: Towards a Development Compact', *EPW*, 33(33 and 34): 2233–39.

Sarkar, Sumit (1999) 'Conversions and Politics of Hindu Right', *EPW*, 26(26 June–2 July): 1691–1700.

Sathyamurthy, T.V. (ed.), (1996a) *Class Formation and Political Transformation in Post-colonial India*, Vol. 4. Delhi: Oxford University Press.

——— (1996b) 'Centralised State Power and Decentralised Politics: Case of India', *EPW*, 31(13): 835–43.

——— (1996c) (ed.) *Region, Religion, Caste, Gender and Culture in Contemporary India*. New Delhi: Oxford University Press.

Schnaiberg, Allen (1970) 'Measuring Modernism: Theoretical and Empirical Exploration', *American Journal of Sociology*, 76: 399–425 .

Seigal, S.M. (1956) 'The Relationship of Hostility to Authoritarianism', *Journal of Abnormal and Social Psychology*, 52: 368–72.

Seligman, Edwin (ed.) (1948) *Encyclopedia of Social Sciences*. New York: MacMillan.

Sen, Amartya (1979) 'Equality for What', Janner Lecture on Human Values, Stanford University, 1979. Reprinted in Amartya Sen (1982) *Choice, Welfare and Measurement*. Cambridge, MA: Harvard University Press.

——— (1997) 'Our Culture: Satyajit Ray and the Art of Universalism', *The New Republic*, 1 April: 27–31.

Sengupta, Chandan and **M.N. Roy** (1996) 'Sociological Impact of Total Literacy Campaign: The Case of Midnapore', *EPW*, 31(9): 483–88.

Shah, G. (1970) 'Communal Riots in Gujarat—Report of the Preliminary investigation', *EPW*. Annual Number: 187–200.

——— (1986) 'Decentralised Planning in a Centralised Economy: A Study of Sarvodaya Programmes in a Taluka' in Peter Robb (ed.) *Rural South Asia: Linkages, Change and Development*. New Delhi: Segment Books.

——— (1990) *Social Movements in India: A Review of Literature*. New Delhi: Sage.

Shankar, P. (1966) 'Education and Caste Hindu Attitudes of the Harijans', *Psychologia*, 9(1): 49–52.

Sharma, M.L. (1969) 'A Comparative Study of Organisational Climates of Government Secondary School and Private Secondary School of Churu District, Rajasthan', *Journal of Educational Research & Extension*, 3: 120–26.

Sheth, D.L. (1971) 'Partisanship and Political Development', *EPW*, 6(3, 4, and 5): 260–73.

———— (1975) 'Structure of Indian Radicalism', *EPW*, 10(5, 6 and 7): 319–34.

———— (1996) 'Changing Terms of Elite Discourse: The Case of Reservation for Other Backward Classes' in T.V. Sathyamurthy (1996a).

Shills, Edward (1966) 'Modernization of Higher Education' in M. Weiner (1966), *Modernization*, New York: The Basic Books Inc. pp. 81–97.

Shiva, Vandana (1989) 'Ecology, Equity and Self-reliance' in Ponna Vignaraja and A. Kamal Hussain (eds.) *The Challenge in South Asia: Development, Democracy and Regional Cooperation*, New Delhi: Sage. pp. 75–87.

Sills, D.L. (ed.) (1968) *International Encyclopedia of Social Sciences*, Vol. 13. New York: The MacMillan Co. and The Free Press.

Singh, A.K. (1971) 'Alienation and Social Change in India'. Paper presented at the Trans-national Symposium on Social Psychological Dimensions of Social Change at the American Psychological Association's Convention, Washington, D.C. 3–7 September.

Sinha, A.K.P. and **R.N.P. Sinha** (1960) 'A Study of Prejudice Among University Students', *Indian Journal of Psychology*, 35: 151–66.

Sinha, A.K.P. and **Upadhyaya, O.P.** (1962) 'Eleven Ethnic Groups on Social Distance Scale', *The Journal of Social Psychology*, 57: 48–59.

Sinha, Dipankar (1999) 'Indian Democracy: Exclusion and Communication', *EPW*, 34(32): 3320–36.

Sinha, G.S. and **R.C. Sinha** (1967) 'Exploration in Caste Stereotypes', *Social Forces*, 47(40): 42–47.

Sinha, J.B.P. (1974) 'From Alienation to Activism', Paper presented at the International Congress of Applied Psychology, Montreal, Canada.

Sinha, Sudha Rani and **J.B.P. Sinha** (1974) 'Campus Activism as a Function of a Nation Among Students', *Journal of Social and Economic Studies*, 2(2): 75–85.

Smith, D.H. and **A. Inkeles** (1966) 'The OM Scale: A Comparative Social Psychological Measure of Modernity', *Sociometry*, (Dec.).

Smith, Wilfred Cantwell (1965) *Modernisation of Traditional Society*. New Delhi: Asia Publishing House.

Srinivas, M.N. (1971) *Social Change in Modern India*. Berkeley: University of California Press.

Srivastava et al. (1967) 'Gujarat Agitation: A Study of Attitudes and Participation of People', *ATIRA*, Ahmedabad: 1–10.

Srivastava, P.K., **S. Sinha** and **U.C. Jain** (1971) 'Some Correlates of Alienation among Indian Female Students', *Indian Journal of Psychology*, 46(4): 395–98.

Sumner, W.G. (1906) *Folkways*. New York: Mentor Book.

Thapar, Romilla, Harbans Mukhia and **Vipin Chandra** (1977) *Communalism and Writing of Indian History*. Second Edition. New York: People's Publishing House.

Thorlind, Robert (1998) *Decentralisation of Local Government Performance: Questioning the Civil Society/Social Capital Paradigm through a Comparison of Different Types of Politicisation in West Bengal and Bangladesh*. Upasala: Nodiac Institute for Asian Studies.

Tornquist, Olle, P.K. Michel Tharakan (1996) 'Democratisation and Attempts to Renew the Radical Political Development Project: The Case of Kerala', *EPW*, 31(28–30): 28–30.

Tornquist, Olle (1999) *Politics and Development.* New Delhi: Sage.

UNICEF (1999) *State of the World's Children 1999.* New York: Oxford University Press.

Vidhyarthi, L.P. (1971) 'Approaches to the Problem of Integration of Tribals in India', in L.P. Vidhyarthi (ed.) *Integration in India.* Bombay: Asian Studies Press.

Warkov, Seymour, and **A.M. Greeley** (1966) 'Parochial School Origins and Educational Achievement', *American Sociological Review,* 31(3): 406–14.

Warner, W.I. et al. (1949) *Social Class in America.* Chicago: Science Research Associate.

Weiner, Myron (1966) *Modernisation: The Dynamic of Growth.* New York: Basic Books Inc.. .

Wells, Allam (1972) 'Mass Violence in India since 1960', *The Indian Political Science Review,* 7(2): 123.

Williams, Robin M. Jr. (1960) *American Society: A Sociological Interpretation.* New York: Alford A. Knopf.

World Bank (1997) *World Development Report 1997: The State in a Changing World.* New York: Oxford University Press.

Xaxa, Vierginius (1999) 'Transformation Tribes in India: Terms of Discourse', *EPW,* 24(12–18 June): 1519–24.

Yadav, Yogendra (1999) 'India's Third Electoral System (1989–99)', *EPW,* (34–35): 2393–99.

Index

202 ➤ Work, Democracy and Development

leadership styles and values, 26, 92, 93, 120, 123, 124, 132; democratic, 161–62; dominative, 105–6, 108, 119, 124, 125, 126, 127, 129, 134, 137, 139, 145–46, 155, 156, 159; educative, 105, 108, 110, 114–15, 116, 134; motivating empowering, 104–5, 108, 110, 113–14, 115, 116, 123, 124, 126, 127, 129, 134, 137, 144, 159, 161; problem-solving, 116

liberalism, 48, 86
liberalisation, 159

mass mobilisation, 19, 32, 34, 140, 142, 149, 155, 160
mental health, 135–36
misanthropism, 55, 56, 164
modernity, 32, 34, 41, 47, 49, 52, 56, 59; psychological, in children, 61, 64; and social prejudice, 48, 74–75
motivation, motivational needs, 93, 99, 117–18, 119, 120, 129
motivating empowering leadership values. *See* leadership styles values, motivating empowering
Mumbai riots, 1992, 24
Muslim children: socio-political attitudes, 76, 80–81, 82, 83, 88
Muslim League, 23

Narayanan, K.R., 151
Narmada Bachao Andolan, 19
Non-government development organisation (NGDO), 28, 33

openness, 47, 48, 55, 56, 166
oppression, 22, 27
organisation, 31–32

panchayati raj institutions, implementation, 17, 28
parochiality: at home, 73; in school management, 69, 70, 71, 73, 87, 88, 147
participation, 99, 117, 119, 134, 135, 142, 146, 151, 154, 160
paternalistic values, 119
people's movement. *See* mass mobilisation

perceptions, 32, 33
personal achievements, 117, 118, 120, 129, 131
personal efficacy, 98, 99, 105, 106, 107, 108, 109, 110, 113, 115, 116, 117, 120–21, 131, 145–46, 155, 160, 161
Phule, Jyotirao, 20
policy documents, 93
populism, 28
poverty, 18, 92
power equations and system, 19, 140
powerlessness, 27, 30, 98, 99, 112, 134, 155, 159
privatisation, 26, 159

Ranchi Riot Enquiry Commission (1967–71), 38
Rashtriya Swayamsevak Sangh (RSS), 23
Reasoning, 15, 120
Reflective: action, 93, 95, 98, 99, 113, 117; efficacy, 121; thinking, 120, 135, 137, 145, 154–55, 160, 161
reliability, 102–6
religious: conflicts, 23; dogmatism, 47, 48, 49, 55, 56
religiosity, religionism, 48, 164
Rentier-Dole tendency, 121, 122, 137, 158
reservation issue, 23
rigidity. *See* status quoism
rumour-mongering, 24, 38

Sanskritisation, 81, 82
sati, glorification, 18
Scheduled Castes and Scheduled Tribes children: social mobility, 84–85, 88; socio-political attitudes, 76, 80–81, 82, 83; social learning, 83–84
school and children, 67–68; attitudes and values, 147–48;–, authoritarianism, 65; communalisation, 66–67; social learning, 86–87; social prejudice, 65; socialisation, 63–64, 87
secularism, secularisation, 31, 41, 47, 49, 56, 66, 69, 70, 74, 86; of children's attitude, 70, 71, 72–74; vs. communalism, 60–61, 65
self-esteem, 98, 99, 117, 125, 135–36, 137, 154, 159, 161, 162

About the Author

Prayag Mehta has held various academic and administrative positions during his career, including Director, School Guidance, Surat; Professor of Research, Indian Institute of Mass Communication, New Delhi; and Director, National Labour Institute, New Delhi. He was also Associate Professor at the NCERT and Professor of Psychology at Udaipur University. Presently, he is working with the Participation and Development Centre, New Delhi.

Professor Mehta has been a Visiting Lecturer at the School of Education, Harvard University and UNIDO consultant at the Hungarian Institute of Building Economy, Budapest. He has worked with several UN agencies abroad and with central government departments and non-governmental development organisations at home. He has published many research papers and books including *A Psychological Strategy for Alternative Human Development: India's Performance since Independence; Education, Participation and Empowerment: Studies in Human Development; Social Achievement Motivation: Values, Needs and Work Organisation;* and *Bureaucracy, Organisational Behaviour and Development.*